OWN YOUR BRAND, OWN YOUR CAREER

The Strategic Guide to Building an Authentic Personal Brand That Accelerates Your Success

By Andy Storch and Mike Kim

ANDY STORCH & MIKE KIM

OWN YOUR BRAND

OWN YOUR CAREER

THE STRATEGIC GUIDE TO BUILDING AN AUTHENTIC PERSONAL BRAND THAT ACCELERATES YOUR SUCCESS

ENDORSEMENTS

"*Own Your Brand, Own Your Career is a masterclass in personal branding and career ownership. Packed with actionable strategies and real-world examples, you'll come away with the tools to take control of your brand and future.*"

May Busch
Former COO of Morgan Stanley Europe and Founder of Career Mastery®

"*In the age of AI, it will become even harder to stand out and differentiate your brand and your skills from others. This book provides a practical guide to help you advance in your career and in your personal life. Your brand is who you are— shape it with purpose to stay relevant in today's world.*"

Amit Parmar
CEO of Cliquify

"*Most people will spend 80,000 hours working so they can one day quit to do what they love. That's not just tragic, it's backwards. Own Your Brand, Own Your Career isn't just about becoming more popular or chasing money, it's a step-by-step playbook to discovering and communicating who you are and why you're here so you can start living a life you love now. Thank you, Andy and Mike!*"

Travis Dommert
SVP of Talent at OneDigital and Keynote Speaker

"*Andy Storch and Mike Kim have written a timely, practical, and inspiring guide for anyone serious about taking charge of their future. Own Your Brand, Own Your Career isn't just another book on professional development—it's a playbook for building an authentic brand, navigating change with confidence, and creating the career you deserve. With real-world wisdom and actionable steps, Andy and Mike give you the tools to stop drifting, take ownership, and design a life and career by choice, not by chance.*"

Garry Ridge
Chairman Emeritus, WD-40 Company; The Culture Coach; and USA Today Bestselling Author of Any Dumb Ass Can Do It

"In a world where the line between personal and professional success is more intertwined than ever, Andy Storch and Mike Kim deliver a powerful roadmap to owning both. Own Your Brand, Own Your Career is a wake-up call for anyone ready to stop drifting and start designing a life and career on purpose. Their insights will help you clarify who you are, what you stand for, and how to make your unique mark in the world. This is a must-read for anyone serious about building a life and career they truly love."

Jairek Robbins
Performance Coach and Bestselling Author of Live It!

"Finally, a book that demystifies personal branding for professionals who want to grow within their organizations. Practical, empowering, and refreshingly real."

Julie Winkle Giulioni
Author of Promotions Are SO Yesterday and Help Them Grow or Watch Them Go

"In today's fast-changing workplace, your personal brand isn't optional—it's essential. Own Your Brand, Own Your Career gives you the roadmap to stand out, stay relevant, and create opportunities on your own terms. Packed with practical strategies and real-world examples, this book will help you take control of your career instead of waiting for someone else to do it. If you want to thrive in the modern world of work, start by reading this book."

Kevin Kruse
New York Times Bestselling Author of Great Leaders Have No Rules and 15 Secrets Successful People Know About Time Management

"Own Your Brand, Own Your Career is a must-read for professionals who want to take ownership of their growth and stand out in today's evolving workplace. As an HR leader, I've seen firsthand how Andy Storch empowers individuals and organizations to embrace development with intention and authenticity. Andy has been a trusted thought partner and champion of talent development for years, and this book is a powerful extension of his mission to help people thrive."

Ryan Calderone
Director of Talent Development at Amica Insurance

"Employees building a personal brand and creating content is a non-negotiable in today's world—it signals psychological safety and trust, which every organization needs to thrive. That's why Own Your Brand, Own Your Career is more than just a book—it's part of a powerful movement. It empowers individuals to own their voice, tell their story, and show up with authenticity. If you want to create a culture where people feel seen, heard, and valued—start by handing them this book."

Darren McKee
Founder of Darren McKee Co. & 531 Social

"As someone passionate about empowering talent and helping people grow in their careers, I see Own Your Brand, Own Your Career as a timely and strategic guide. It challenges readers to think beyond roles and résumés and instead build a purposeful, visible brand rooted in authenticity. This book is packed with practical insights for anyone looking to grow their influence, increase their impact, and take ownership of their future."

Dr. Keith Keating
Author of The Trusted Learning Advisor and Hidden Value

"Owning your own story is what gives your brand its power and individuality. Own Your Brand, Own Your Career helps to make that possible. This book shows you how to stand out, with intention, clarity, and courage. As someone who has built an online community by showing up honestly—messy, imperfect, but with heart and good intentions—I can confidently say this is the playbook you need for building a career that's felt, not just seen. Read it. Own it. Then watch the magic start to unfold."

Lea Turner
Founder of The HoLT, LinkedIn Rebel, and Community Builder

"In Own Your Brand, Own Your Career, my friends Andy Storch and Mike Kim break down exactly how to take ownership of the way others perceive your value in a way that has never been so easy to read and likeable. In this book, they've provided highly actionable and specific strategies that apply whether you're climbing the corporate ladder, pivoting careers, or building your own practice from scratch."

Lauren V. Davis
Personal Brand Strategist and Coach

"How does someone like me, living on the other side of the world, know of Andy Storch and Mike Kim? Because they show up consistently, boldly, authentically, and prolifically. Own Your Brand, Own Your Career is full of lessons and relatable and funny stories that will inspire you to create your own incredible opportunities and brand."

Leanne Hughes
Author of The 2-Hour Workshop Blueprint and Host of First Time Facilitator and Leanne on Demand

"Own Your Brand, Own Your Career is a wake-up call for professionals ready to define their own path. With the same honesty and practical wisdom I value in Human Resources, this book reminds us that building a career is about owning your story and showing up authentically."

Cory Sanford
Author of HR You Kidding Me?: Surprisingly Simple Steps to Unlock the Power of People

"Own Your Brand, Own Your Career is an inspirational and practical guide to writing your own narrative, charting your own path, and ultimately architecting your career. Both Andy and Mike have not only done this in their own careers, but they have also helped countless others to do the same."

JP Elliott
Founder and Host of the Future of HR

"If you're serious about standing out—whether in your organisation or as a leader in your own right—Own Your Brand, Own Your Career isn't just another book. It's THE handbook."

Bob Gentle
LeaderBrand Business Strategist and Coach

"Own Your Brand, Own Your Career is a powerful and practical guide for anyone ready to step into their full potential. As someone who supports women in building unapologetic personal brands, I appreciate how this book encourages readers to stop hiding, own their strengths, and take control of their career paths."

Gemma Stow
Executive Coach and Visibility Expert

"Your personal brand is not just who you are online, it's who you are and how you manifest serendipity in your career and life. Own Your Brand, Own Your Career gives you the framework to build a voice that attracts opportunities, relationships, and growth, all while staying true to yourself."

Liam Darmody
Personal Brand Strategist, Founder of Liam's Brand Stand and LinkedIn Creator

"In a rapidly changing world where influence is key, Andy and Mike have created an expert guidance system to create your personal brand in Own Your Brand, Own Your Career. A witty guide to the big (and small) changes that you can make to create, revamp or continue building your personal brand so that you can cultivate influence and impact throughout your career.

This book is a definite must-read for anyone who has been confused about what personal brands really bring to the table and will help you create a personal brand that is meaningful and true to who you are!"

Jessica Lorimer
Founder of Selling to Corporate ®

To Cortney, Lucy, and Teddy, who are always there with me. You give me purpose.

To my parents who always let me be who I am, even if they didn't understand it.

And to the many mentors and friends who showed me the way and helped me build my personal brand. I've learned and benefited so much from these amazing people and from investing in myself over the years.

-Andy

To my mom, who never once asked me to get a good job.

Whether I wanted to be a comic book artist, a musician, in ministry, or whatever it is I do now, you were always supportive of my path and knew how I was wired.

I love you, Mom.

-Mike

CONTENTS

START HERE

It's hard to feel really fulfilled in life when you hate your job.

We know that might sound obvious, but think about it for a moment. You spend roughly a third or more of your waking hours working. Probably more for most people. That's more time than you probably spend with your family, and definitely more time than you spend on hobbies, travel, or pretty much anything else you might enjoy. If those hours are filled with dread, frustration, or simply going through the motions, a massive chunk of your life can feel wasted.

Too many talented people are stuck in jobs they've learned to tolerate, compartmentalize, or outright hate. They drag themselves to work Monday morning, count down to Friday afternoon, and repeat the cycle for far too long. They tell themselves this is just how work is supposed to feel and that expecting more is naive or unrealistic.

We beg to differ.

While work doesn't need to be your whole purpose in life, it can absolutely be a meaningful part of it. Work should be something you enjoy, learn from, and grow as a result of.

Here's what we've learned after years of helping people build personal brands and transform careers: there's an opportunity like never before right now to get ahead in your career. When new trends or technology come along, they often create waves and vacuums for people to accelerate their careers because everything is so new.

When we were in college, it was the internet that cracked open new pathways for career success. Today, it certainly seems AI is the catalyst. The landscape is shifting, traditional career paths are being rewritten, and those who understand how to position themselves strategically can make incredible leaps forward.

The timing of us partnering together isn't coincidental. We've been hard at work for two years on this book. In an effort to bring our best foot forward, we've done speaking engagements all across the world, both on our own and together, led workshops on the concepts within, and called on the best of our friends and most respected colleagues within both of our networks to bring you actionable, practical insights that can really help you in your career.

We chose to self-publish because we want to deliver the most current and relevant information while the window of opportunity is still wide open. In a rapidly-changing landscape like this, waiting another two years for traditional publishing timelines would mean you'd be getting yesterday's advice for tomorrow's challenges. That's not what you need.

Admittedly, we both really enjoy what we do for a living, and we've been fortunate enough to meet lots of people who enjoy what they do for a living. What we've noticed is that they're just happier; they're more impactful. People who like what they do tend to make better money, and often in ways that are more aligned with their lifestyles. They use their talents and gifts more fully, and generally make life better for their loved ones and colleagues.

It's inspiring to meet people who love what they do. We're naturally drawn to passion. As avid sports fans, neither of us like to watch games where the players are just going through the motions and collecting a paycheck. We want to see the ones who find joy and purpose in the game. The same is true in the workplace: when you meet someone who works from a place of alignment with what they're doing, they're magnetic. You can feel their energy and expertise, as well as their authentic enthusiasm.

That's what we want for you.

Andy brings deep expertise in career development and professional growth. He's the author of *Own Your Career Own Your Life*, a keynote speaker who's delivered over 50 presentations, and the host of the Talent Development Hot Seat podcast with over 500 episodes and 500,000 downloads. He's also the founder of the Talent Development Think Tank conference and community. Andy specializes in helping corporate professionals own their careers, prepare for the future, and achieve their goals with intention and strategy.

Mike came out of a career in marketing and has spent

years helping executives, experts, and entrepreneurs build authentic personal brands that create opportunities and accelerate careers. He understands how to help talented people get noticed, get heard, and get ahead by learning to communicate their value clearly and consistently. As the author of the *Wall Street Journal* bestselling book *You Are the Brand*, Mike has been in this industry for over a decade and witnessed what endures and what are just fads.

Together, we've seen something powerful: combining personal branding and career development leads to success that compounds on itself. When you know how to build your brand and own your career simultaneously, you get ahead faster, you have more control, and you're more likely to head in a direction that actually fulfills you.

This book will show you how.

Through most of this book, we'll write from a unified voice, sharing our combined insights and perspectives. In some sections and chapters, however, one of us will take the lead when drawing from our specific areas of expertise or personal experiences. This approach allows us to give you the most authentic and practical guidance possible.

You'll learn how to identify and articulate your unique value, build authentic relationships that matter, create content that showcases your expertise, navigate career transitions strategically, and position yourself for opportunities that align with who you are and where you want to go. You'll discover how to leverage LinkedIn effectively, how to interview with confidence, how to think like an intrapreneur within your current company, and how to develop the human skills that will matter even more as AI transforms the workplace.

Most importantly, you'll learn how to stop waiting for permission, recognition, or the "perfect" opportunity, and start creating the career you actually want.

As you read, we hope you'll go beyond merely consuming these ideas, and actually try to apply them. Each chapter includes practical exercises and actionable strategies you can implement immediately. We've also created a free workbook with all the exercises compiled in one place, which you can download at ownyourbrandbook.com.

GET YOUR FREE WORKBOOK

Before you dive into Chapter One, we highly recommend downloading our comprehensive workbook. It contains every exercise from this book in an easy-to-use format, plus bonus templates and reflection prompts you won't find anywhere else. This is your roadmap to building a brand that opens doors and accelerates your career.

Download it now at ownyourbrandbook.com so you can work through the exercises as you read. Trust us—having it ready will make your experience with this book exponentially more valuable.

The career you want is possible. The fulfillment you're seeking is achievable. And the impact you want to make is within reach.

Let's get started.

Andy Storch & Mike Kim

Barcelona, Spain, and Fort Lee, NJ, respectively

CHAPTER ONE:

YOU ALREADY HAVE A BRAND, SO OWN IT

Do you remember your first screen name or social media handle? Both of us were in high school during the early days of the internet when web portals like America Online (AOL), CompuServe, and Netscape were all the rage.

Back then, internet life basically consisted of chat rooms, reading blogs (Xanga, anyone?), and chatting with people through AOL Instant Messenger—or AIM, for short.

AIM was a messaging app that became the precursor to the direct messaging features found on most social media platforms we use today. One summer, all of my (Mike) friends caught the AIM bug and everyone seemed to have an account. Andy was doing the same. AIM was the place to be!

I scrounged through my family's mail to track down one of the free CDs that America Online was sending out in those days. I grabbed our telephone cord, plugged it into the computer, and fired up that snail-paced modem ready to join the party that was happening on AIM.

Suddenly I stopped completely in my tracks, my face frozen by what I saw on the screen.

I had to create a username for my AIM account.

Laugh if you will, but I'm positive I'm not the only person who freaked out at the idea of creating my own username. Maybe you had the same feeling when you first got on Instagram or some other social network. It can feel like a big decision, as if our handle is a reflection of us.

I must have stared at the screen for at least half an hour trying to come up with something cool and witty. My username had to be cool because, you know, I had friends to impress.

After what seemed like an eternity, I came up with the perfect username. It would be powerful! It would project strength! It would sound unique! It would be a clever play on my first name, and girls would surely bombard me with requests for dates! My AIM username would be...

Mikovitch!

(Stop laughing.)

Things didn't work out the way I imagined. In fact, they completely backfired. All of my friends thought it was the dumbest username ever. One of my buddies asked if I was trying to sound Russian, and from that point on whenever I saw my friends in person, they greeted me with a military salute, "Greetings, Comrade Mikovitch!"

The final moment of humiliation was when a girl I

really liked said she had an even better username for me: "Miko*bitch*." I still remember her laughing at me. (Whatever, I'm a grown man now, and she's probably living a miserable exis—oh, never mind.)

Andy's first screenname wasn't too much better. After some long consideration, he decided on the name "Astrostorch" which didn't seem to impress many people either, but he stuck with it for several years.

We may not have realized it back then, but choosing a username was an early exercise in shaping how others perceive us. Today, part of our attempt to describe this phenomenon is known as personal branding.

SO, WHAT IS A PERSONAL BRAND?

As you may know, "branding" stems from the old ranching practice of burning an identifying mark onto livestock with an iron (a "brand"; see also "firebrand"). The concept of branding later expanded into business and marketing to identify products manufactured by a particular company under a particular name.

Josiah Wedgwood, an English potter born in the 1700s, was perhaps the first person who leveraged branding to create a retail empire. After winning a competition hosted by Queen Charlotte, Wedgwood dubbed his pottery "Queen's Ware," opened an exclusive showroom in London for a more affluent market, and pioneered sales practices of "money-back guarantees" and "free delivery."

Whether it has to do with livestock, pottery, cars, or

how we present ourselves online, branding is simply about identity. Personal branding expands the concept of branding to include a person's ideas, expertise, reputation, work style, and personality. For the rest of this book, we'll use this as our framework:

Your personal brand is a public-facing identity made up of your ideas, expertise, reputation, and personality.

In personal branding, we intentionally craft a public identity for a specific purpose. Celebrities do it to sell tickets, entrepreneurs to grow their business, politicians to get elected, and corporate professionals to attract opportunities and advance their careers.

The reality is that you already have a brand, whether you've paid attention to it or not. Think about your colleagues at work. You likely have opinions about each of them: "John is nice, but always late to meetings," or "Lauren goes out of her way to help on projects," or "Kat truly cares about people."

These descriptions reflect the brands people create through their actions, whether intentional or not. Your colleagues are forming such impressions about you, too.

Our friend Dave recently told us a story that highlights this. Dave is in his mid-40s and holds an important leadership role at his company in New York City. Most of his direct reports are in their 20s, creating a bit of a generational gap.

During one of his annual reviews, Dave learned that his colleagues sometimes weren't sure if he was upset and were sometimes hesitant to bring things up to him.

Dave was shocked. Sure, he's a big guy with a voice that fills a room, but he genuinely cares about his team, is known as a great networker, and certainly never intended to seem intimidating. He thought to himself, "How can I change this?"

Dave saw an opportunity and decided to start by simply changing the signature on his emails. Email is his company's primary communication channel so he figured if anything, people would be seeing emails from him multiple times a day during the workweek.

Dave started signing off on his emails with "warmly," and noticed a surprising change around the way his team interacted with him. Some of his colleagues would even joke with him, "Hey Dave, have a great day! I say that warmly," then give the old point and wink.

Dave's small adjustment helped bridge a bit of the generational gap and softened his presence, leading to a more cohesive and comfortable team environment. "Warmly," dare we say, has become a part of his personal brand.

Can such a small shift really make that big of a difference? In short, yes. We live in a world where these small touches matter more than ever before. Andy's email signature always starts "with gratitude," and he often ends his podcast episodes expressing appreciation. The underlying message: he wants to be known as someone who is grateful and inspires others to live with the same mindset.

Whether it's a simple email signoff or a comprehensive content strategy, these examples prove it's possible to shape how people perceive you and be intentional about how you come across. This has never been more important in the world of work than it is today.

In earlier generations, the popular advice was to put your head down, work hard, and don't rock the boat. Maybe you could make a good impression with quality work on a few significant projects and those wins could sustain your career. But in today's "what have you done for me lately" world, where even spearheading a big win doesn't guarantee job security, intentionally building a personal brand can help you grow a sustainable career through small, consistent actions rather than one or two big projects. If you stick with this over time, you can leverage the power of your personal brand to give you more agency in your professional life.

"BUT I DON'T WANT TO BE AN INFLUENCER"

We hear you—and if you do, we have no issue with that either. Both of us have worked hard to build our personal brands through books, podcasts, blogs, social media content, and networking so we totally appreciate how much hard work goes into this stuff. But we don't think of ourselves as "influencers"—we just try to be influential to the people around us.

Much of the negative sentiment around influencer culture stems from the inauthenticity of what we often see online. The personal brand space often plays out in two ways. The first group of people sells a false version of themselves, thinking that image or perception alone will get them the results they seek. These folks don't realize that no one owes anyone attention; we have to earn it. (If you've ever seen a "guru" online shooting a "crushing goals" video in what appears to be their stunning mansion, only for you later to discover the house was actually rented on Airbnb for the recording, you probably know what we mean.)

The flip side of presenting a false version of yourself is oversharing in the name of authenticity. These people post online about their issues, sometimes revealing a lot more than what's even comfortable for us to read about as strangers. It's as if these people are trying to sell their struggles instead of offering solutions or value. Like a car wreck, this approach can definitely garner attention—but only because people can't help but look. The attention is short-lived and doesn't build the kind of lasting, positive reputation that actually helps your career.

So, what are we to do?

We start by examining how we're showing up: at work, in our personal lives, online, and in our interactions with others.

Here's a simple question that can serve as a litmus test: "Can you build a campfire around what you're sharing?" By that we mean: Is there warmth? Are you a light in a dark place? Are you building something that is inviting to others? Are you someone who others want to invite into their companies, onto their projects, into their boardrooms, in front of their teams, or into their lives?

While it may sound like we're telling you to build a brand, we're actually challenging you to do something bigger. Don't just build a brand: *become* the brand. Take ownership of your growth and do the hard work required to become the person you're trying to "sell" or portray to others. We promise you that you won't be on your journey very long before you have to confront your own dissonance. You can only "fake it till you make it" so long. So embrace integrity, and welcome growth. Step up and be your best self—it will make everything easier.

Careers today just don't look anything like they did 20 years ago. The U.S. Department of Labor reports that individuals born in the latter years of the baby boom held an average of 12.7 jobs from ages 18 to 56, and that number is projected to increase for younger generations.

The reality is simple: jobs change, you evolve, and the skills required for success are constantly shifting. This is exactly why personal branding matters more than ever. In a world where career stability is no longer guaranteed, your reputation becomes your security.

In a recent survey by the American Psychology Association, 93% of people said it's important to have a job where they feel the work has meaning. But the things that give you meaning can change over time.

Sometimes the work is just terrible and you need change. Other times, change materializes unexpectedly, like discovering a new passion that causes you to change careers completely. Or, other times, life changes like having a family can shift what's truly important to you.

Regularly taking inventory of what matters to you is one of the best ways to not just be more intentional about your personal brand, but to find work that actually makes you feel alive.

THE PERSONAL BRAND 3 (PB3)

If you've been at your job long enough to wonder why you do what you do, you might be losing sight of what you really want in life. The thing is, we don't always know what we want, but it's easy for us to know what we *don't* want. If you've ever wrestled with what to eat for dinner or what kind of outfit you wanted to buy, you know that feeling when someone offers something and you immediately say "no." Sometimes it's easier to look at what you do *not* want rather than what you *do* want.

To help draw out what's inside, we propose three simple questions we call the Personal Brand 3, or PB3 for short. (Mike is from Jersey, so please excuse the salty language.) We're intentionally using emotional language here because all too often, we play things safe. Now is not the time for that. This exercise is just for you, so let loose with no editing or filtering.

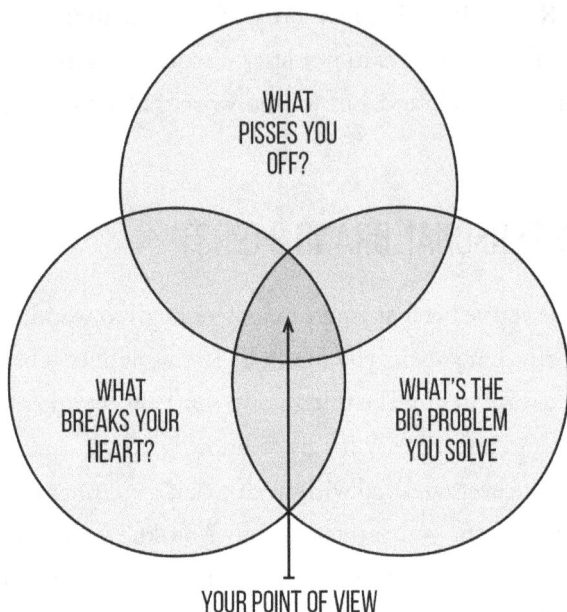

YOUR POINT OF VIEW

1. WHAT PISSES YOU OFF?

This question is about the injustice you see in the world, and can include things that frustrate or annoy you and drive you to want to make a change.

If "injustice" sounds too big and grand, start with the things that at least frustrate and annoy you. Maybe you hate your long commute because you value time with family over a prestigious office location. Maybe it's working for companies that say they value work-life balance but expect you to answer emails at 10 PM—revealing that boundaries matter more to you than appearing "always available." Maybe you're frustrated when leaders take credit for your ideas, showing you need recognition and intellectual honesty in your workplace. Or maybe being passed over for promotions despite great work tells you you need more transparent career advancement and merit-based decisions.

As you list these frustrations, you may start seeing patterns that reveal a fuller picture of what you want to fight for or against, and how your professional life might play a role in that.

2. WHAT BREAKS YOUR HEART?

This question touches on your compassion and empathy. What issues or situations cause you emotional pain? Who do you care about? What causes, if any, do you care about both inside and outside of work?

Maybe it breaks your heart when you see talented colleagues leave because they can't afford childcare on their salary—revealing that you care about economic equity and family support. Maybe you're deeply affected when you watch older workers get pushed out during layoffs, which would show that you value experience and age diversity. Perhaps it hurts to see your company's environmental impact; this implies that sustainability matters to your sense of purpose. Or, maybe you're moved when you see how your product genuinely helps customers solve real problems, telling you that meaningful impact drives your satisfaction more than just hitting revenue targets.

Thinking about these things helps you identify what you care about deeply and what you might want to work towards improving or solving in your career.

3. WHAT PROBLEM(S) ARE YOU TRYING TO SOLVE?

This question aims to uncover a deeper sense of purpose and meaning. What significant challenge or problem do you want to address through your work? If you could wave a magic wand and change something about the world (not just your world), what would it be?

Maybe you're driven to solve communication breakdowns because you've seen how much damage poor communication causes in teams—revealing that you're meant to build bridges between people and ideas. Perhaps you're passionate about making complex technology accessible to everyday users, showing that democratizing knowledge and tools drives your sense of purpose. Maybe you want to help small businesses compete with larger corporations, which says that you value leveling the playing field and supporting underdogs. Or perhaps you're focused on helping people make better financial decisions because you've witnessed how financial stress destroys lives; this could tell you that empowering people through education is your calling.

Understanding this can help you align your career with a higher mission or deeper calling.

Have fun with this! It's normal to feel a bit foggy. Don't hold back. Don't filter yourself. Draw the emotions out and get it down on paper. You can always refine it later.

***

Once you've worked through these three questions, take a step back and look at what you've uncovered. The patterns that emerge—the things that frustrate you, move you, and drive you—are clues to who you are and what you're meant to contribute.

You have a brand, so own it.

Own your values. Own your wants. Own your preferences. Own the responsibility to become the person who can step into, earn, and attract those things.

As you do this kind of self-work, you become better. You grow and develop into someone others are naturally drawn to—someone they want to work with, learn from, and support. You begin to take more intentional control of your career story and, in many ways, your personal life too.

The work isn't always easy, but it's worth it. The best part is that you get to start wherever you are, with whatever you have, right now.

At the end of each chapter, we'll provide action items to help you apply what we've discussed. Again, we recommend that you download our exercise book PDF from our website at ownyourbrandbook.com. Please either download the workbook, or grab a notebook, to work through the following exercises:

REFLECTION PROMPTS

Use these questions to reflect on the themes of this chapter.

1. What was your first screen name or handle?

What were you trying to signal about yourself at the time? What does that choice say about how you wanted to be perceived?

2. What small actions shape how others see you?

Think of something subtle, like your email signoff, tone in meetings, or how you respond to messages. What might that be communicating?

3. Can you build a campfire around what you're putting out?

Are you creating warmth and light in your presence, or are you unknowingly keeping people at a distance?

THE PERSONAL BRAND 3 (PB3)

Use these questions to draw out what matters most to you.

- **What pisses you off?**

What frustrates you or feels unfair? What values are being violated when that happens?

- **What breaks your heart?**

What issues move you emotionally? Who or what do you care about—at work or in the world?

- **What problems are you trying to solve?**

What challenges do you feel called to take on through your work, creativity, or leadership?

PATTERN FINDER

Look across your PB3 answers. What themes show up more than once? What do these patterns suggest about your values, motivations, or future direction?

Try to make it a habit to reflect regularly on these questions and others to continue to refine and build your personal brand.

CHAPTER TWO:

FROM DRIFT TO DIRECTION: FINDING PURPOSE IN THE WORK YOU DO

In the last chapter, we asked you to dig into what frustrates you, breaks your heart, and what problems you want to solve. If you're like most people who work through that exercise, you probably discovered something interesting: you know a lot more about what you *don't* want than what you *do* want.

That's completely normal—and actually useful. Sometimes the clearest path forward starts with identifying what to move away from. But at some point, you have to turn toward something. That's what this chapter is about.

Remember that statistic from Chapter One? 93% of people say it's important to have a job where they feel the work has meaning. We're not necessarily talking about finding your "life's calling" written in the stars. We're talking about the very practical reality that most of us spend roughly a third of our waking hours at work. If that time feels empty or misaligned with who you are, it can affect everything else.

Both of us have been where you might be right now: knowing what we didn't want but feeling foggy about what we actually wanted. What we learned is that a clear idea doesn't usually arrive as a lightning bolt and that the path is rarely straightforward.

Growing up in Orlando, Florida, Andy was completely convinced he'd be a professional baseball player.

"My bedroom walls were covered in posters of Chicago Cubs stars, especially Ryne Sandberg, the all-star second baseman. From age six to fourteen, baseball was everything. I lived it, breathed it, dreamed it. And my dream was to play professionally one day like my heroes.

"There was just one problem: I wasn't putting in nearly enough work. Sure, I played Little League baseball and went to practice and played in the games. But there was never any real thought about how to get better or achieve my ultimate goals. No seeking out coaching or putting in extra reps. The assumption was that showing up would be enough.

"When tryouts came around for my high school team, I didn't even go because I knew I wouldn't make the team. That was it—my dream of playing ball ended. Staring at those Ryne Sandberg posters, I felt like I'd let myself down. But instead of learning from it, I just... moved on.

"Looking back, that moment wasn't just about baseball, it was a pattern in my life. When I got to college, I chose civil engineering as my major. Roads, bridges, and learning how cities worked had always been fascinating. Math and physics had always come easily, so engineering felt like a logical fit. But when I had to take chemistry, which *didn't* come naturally, I struggled and eventually I gave up. I didn't find a better path to change my major; I just didn't have a clear plan or purpose. I wasn't owning it.

"That choice set off a series of others, none of them especially thoughtful. I graduated with a degree I wasn't passionate about, took the first decent job offer I got—a management training program at Walgreens—and hated it. I quit after a few months, bounced between jobs that didn't stick, and eventually moved to California with my wife, Cortney, while still trying to figure out what I wanted to do.

"It took almost a decade of drifting before something finally clicked. In my early 30s, I landed a consulting role that changed a lot for me. I started working with mentors, learning about my strengths, and building relationships, and discovered my strengths. That job gave me a snapshot of what it felt like to do work I actually enjoyed.

"Then I got into personal development and started doing more learning and reflecting, taking more ownership of my career, and really discovering my purpose in life and the work that gave me the most fulfillment. That was absolutely *huge*, but if I'm being honest, it could've happened a lot sooner if I had been more intentional earlier on—which is exactly why I wrote my first book, *Own Your*

Career, Own Your Life."

For Mike, the story unfolded differently.

"There's always been this sense that life was meant to be meaningful—not necessarily big, public, or flashy but just something that mattered. That pull showed up early in life, especially through spirituality and religion. Those paths got explored, but over time the structures didn't fit. However, that pull stayed.

"For years, the same question followed me into every job: Is this it? Most of the time, the answer was no. When I was offered a music director position at a large church in Connecticut in my early 30s, I thought that was what I was supposed to do. When that turned out to be the wrong fit too, a much bigger question emerged: If not this... then what?

"There wasn't a clear answer. All that was certain was wanting to live a full life—like that Bon Jovi lyric: "I just wanna live while I'm alive." My desire was to travel, hear people's stories, and contribute to something bigger than myself.

"When I resigned from that role, I moved back to New Jersey and took a part-time job at an after-school academy where I worked just out of college. One day while walking out the door, my boss asked me if I had a moment to do a quality check on an ad for the company.

"All it took was a quick glance: 'Actually, the design isn't good because it's not very clear what you guys are promoting here. This font needs to be bigger, and here the message is a little buried. But most of all, you haven't communicated what value someone is going to get if they enroll their child here.'

"She was astonished because she didn't realize I knew anything about marketing. And in truth, I didn't have formal training. But years of promoting church events, recruiting volunteers, and crafting messages that moved people to action had built those skills without me realizing it.

"She paused for a moment and asked me to sit down. Her words literally changed the course of my life. She said, 'Mike, I want you to take over all of the marketing for the entire company. Name your price.' After a bit of shock, I pulled a number out of the air (it was a lot) and the job was mine.

"Since I didn't have formal marketing education, I devoured every book I could find—authors like Ogilvy, Caples, Schwartz. Reading *Ogilvy on Advertising* made me realize I'd been doing marketing all my life: hosting conferences, promoting albums, crafting messages.

"The company increased its revenue within the first year and my work finally aligned with my drive to help people bring ideas to life. For the first time, purpose wasn't something I was searching for, it was something I was living."

***

If there's one thread that runs through both of our stories, it's this: for a long time, we were just going through the motions. We weren't steering the ship—we were just floating with the current. As the saying goes, "Even a dead fish can go with the flow."

Eventually, we both learned to stop drifting and take ownership of our careers and lives. To get intentional and proactive in figuring out who we are and what we want to do, and then taking action to achieve our goals. This is what ownership is all about—and we know good things will happen if you choose to take control of your career, life, and brand as well. Here's a helpful question to get the gears turning:

Are you living by default or by design?

Living by default happens when you let life happen to you. You show up, maybe you even work hard, but you are not intentional about where you are going. You just follow the path of least resistance or make decisions based on what's in front of you rather than what you really want. It can look like taking a job because it was offered, staying in a role that feels safe but drains you, or letting others define what success means for you.

The alternative is owning your life or living by design. It means defining success on your own terms and making moves that align with your values. You take ownership of your direction, rather than just reacting, and start to align your life in a more purposeful way.

If you've ever felt stuck, chances are you or someone you know has thought, "Just do *something*." It's a common, well-meaning notion. But without clarity, "just doing something" can turn into frantic activity with no real progress and even amplify the confusion. Sure, doing something is usually better than doing nothing at all, and we all need to experiment to find what works. But the pressure to "just do something" can create a low-level anxiety that pushes you into fear-based decisions.

You start to believe you're running out of time, that everyone else is ahead, and that if you don't act now, you'll miss your shot (by the way, if you suffer from constantly comparing yourself to others, you are not alone. Andy wrote a whole chapter about comparison in his first book, *Own Your Career Own Your Life*).

The problem is alignment. You don't need more random action: you need thoughtful action with meaningful direction.

We've each had our fair share of sleepless nights wondering, "What am I going to do with my life? What am I supposed to do? What is my purpose?" When people talk about "purpose," they often use it interchangeably with vision, mission, or goals as if they all mean the same thing. That confusion can make it harder to get a clear idea of what you need, so let's break down a simpler, more practical framework that helps you actually move forward.

PURPOSE, VISION, MISSION, GOALS: A SIMPLER FRAMEWORK

Most people think "finding purpose" is some grand, philosophical journey that requires meditation retreats and journaling in candlelit rooms. If that works for you, great. We both believe in mediation and reflection, but for now we'd like to offer a more actionable path forward. We like to think of Purpose, Vision, Mission, and Goals like a stack that helps you gain clarity in your life and momentum in your career:

- Purpose
- Vision
- Mission
- Goals

Your purpose is the big "why" behind everything you do. It's broad enough to guide you through different seasons of life, but specific enough to give meaning to your work. For example, your purpose might be "to help people reach their potential" or "to help solve complex problems." It's the thing that stays consistent even as your job or career path changes and answers the question "why do you do what you do?" or "why do you want to achieve that goal?"

Your vision is how you see that purpose playing out over time. You might see yourself solving problems as a trusted internal advisor, building solutions as an external consultant, writing and speaking about your expertise, or even teaching others to navigate the challenges you've mastered. The purpose remains the thread, but the vision shapes how you express it.

Your mission (which we should all remember is a military term) is how you bring that vision to life in the short term. You might think of it like a focused campaign:

it's actionable, measurable, and time-bound. Ask any military veteran and they will confirm that there's no such thing as a mission without clear parameters. Missions often change depending on your season or priorities, but they always support your vision. For example, if your vision is to become a Director of Operations, your mission might be to take on a certain number of cross-functional projects, build leadership experience, or earn a certification in project management within the next year.

Your goals are the milestones and achievements along the way. They're the things you can track and measure, like "Lead two cross-functional initiatives this quarter," "Complete my PMP certification by December," or "Have a career development conversation with my manager this month." These help you measure momentum and stay accountable. Clear, specific goals help you know whether your mission is working and if you're moving in the right direction.

THE SNAPSHOT 7: BRINGING YOUR PURPOSE INTO FOCUS

To help you clarify where you are and where you're headed, here's a quick diagnostic we call the Snapshot 7: seven questions that bring your values, energy, and direction into focus. How you answer them will give you a snapshot of where your energy and career are aligned and where you might need to make some changes.

1. If I could design my career from scratch, would it look anything like what I'm doing now?

2. What parts of my work make me feel alive? Which ones drain me?

3. When do I feel most engaged at work?

4. What kind of work makes me forget to check the clock?

5. What problems do I love solving?

6. If I keep going like this for the next five years, will I be proud of where I end up?

7. How do I want people to describe my impact?

You don't have to blow up your career to move it in a more aligned direction. The smarter shifts usually start with small, low-risk experiments. Instead of quitting your job on a whim or going all-in on a new path, test the waters. Shadow someone in a field that interests you. Take on a small freelance project. Enroll in a short course before committing to a full degree program.

When Mike was working in marketing, he asked his company to cover the cost of a training program on running Facebook and Instagram ads. He wasn't sure if he'd enjoy it, but figured it could benefit the company either way. After digging in, he quickly realized that running ads wasn't for him, but the company still gained value from what he learned.

When Andy landed his consulting job, he found that

he really liked planning social events for his co-workers to connect. In retrospect, those moments were the seeds of something much bigger. He didn't know it at the time, but the skills he was building by organizing those team events would later evolve into planning and hosting full-scale conferences and retreats. What started as casual team-building happy hours eventually became a key part of his life's work.

These kinds of micro-experiments let you explore new possibilities, build skills, and gather feedback without betting the farm. Look for adjacent opportunities that allow you to use your existing skills in new contexts or let you stretch into areas of interest.

CONNECTING TO YOUR ORGANIZATION'S BIGGER PURPOSE

Even if your specific role doesn't light a fire in you, sometimes the broader mission of an organization can. For some, that's enough to bring meaning into their day-to-day lives. When your work contributes to something larger, it can feel aligned even if your job title isn't your dream role.

Mike saw this firsthand when he went on a trip to Uganda with the Ugandan Water Project, a nonprofit focused on freeing communities from waterborne disease and poverty. During his visit, he was invited to lead a few seminars with the local team on marketing and branding. Every team member he met had a deep sense of purpose.

They weren't all passionate about water specifically, but they were deeply committed to human dignity. For many of them, working at this organization felt like the most meaningful way to align their personal purpose to their work.

One team member put it best: "I may not be passionate about water forever, but right now this is the best way I know to help our country." That kind of alignment, between personal desire and organizational purpose, is powerful. It turns a job into a calling, even when the tasks themselves are ordinary.

Andy has worked with many corporate professionals over the years, and has found the ones who connect more with their organization's mission or are able to connect what the business does with their own mission or purpose seem to have more passion for their work.

Whether you work for a mission-driven organization like the Ugandan Water Project or a publicly traded company, almost all organizations have a stated purpose—and the more you can connect your own purpose to theirs, the more motivated you'll be to create value and succeed at work.

Most companies don't offer something like this, but that doesn't mean you can't do it yourself. Consider your company's broader purpose and where your role fits in. If that connection doesn't exist, maybe it's time to explore new opportunities.

To wrap up this chapter, let's move from ideas and into action. For now, take a few minutes to answer The Snapshot 7. Don't overthink it, just write down what comes up. Remember, we've put all the rest of the exercises and templates in a free workbook available from ownyourbrandbook.com.

1. If I could design my career from scratch, would it look anything like what I'm doing now?

2. What parts of my work make me feel alive? Which ones drain me?

3. When do I feel most engaged at work?

4. What kind of work makes me forget to check the clock?

5. What problems do I love solving?

6. If I keep going like this for the next five years, will I be proud of where I end up?

7. How do I want people to describe my impact?

Once you've worked through these questions, you'll have a clearer picture of what you want. The next step is learning how to communicate that story to others—which is exactly what we'll tackle in the next chapter.

CHAPTER THREE:
SHAPE YOUR NARRATIVE OR SOMEONE ELSE WILL

Several years ago one of our clients was on a flight to a speaking engagement to promote his latest book. The man sitting in the next seat happened to be reading that very book. The catch? The man didn't know he was sitting next to the author.

Thinking this would be a great opportunity to get some unfiltered feedback, our client asked his seatmate what the book was about. Unfortunately, the man replied with a very weak description of the book, and after some hemming and hawing, simply said something like, "It's really good, you just have to read it," and that he was on his way to hear the author speak at a conference!

Our client was disappointed that one of his avid readers gave such an unpersuasive pitch. He thought that if this guy couldn't convince him to buy his own book, something was wrong.

The client realized it was his job to shape what readers say about his book and how they describe it to others. It was his job to brand the book better. It was his job, as they say in marketing, to shape the narrative. We can't ever control what other people say about us or our work, but we can absolutely influence them by becoming more intentional about our brands and shaping the narrative.

In philosophy and early physics, there's a common saying often attributed to Aristotle: *horror vacui*—commonly stated as "nature abhors a vacuum." The phrase expresses the idea that unfilled spaces go against the laws of nature and that every space needs to be filled with something. If you've ever seen an abandoned building or a crater overrun by vegetation, you get the idea.

This principle applies to narratives and even everyday communication. Think about the last time you called or texted someone close to you and didn't hear back right away. Did your mind start jumping to conclusions? It's easy to assume something's wrong—that they're upset with us or something bad has happened—when in reality, they were probably just busy or hadn't seen the message yet.

We see this at work, too. Say your manager emails you in the morning and asks you to stop by their office before you go home, with no other context or explanation. Your mind starts to wander and often will go to a worst-case scenario: "Am I in trouble? Am I getting fired?" You'd give almost anything to get a hint of what they want to talk to you about. Talk about the longest day ever! In the absence of certainty, people tend to fill the gap with assumptions, and those assumptions are rarely positive.

The same is true for your reputation and personal brand. If you are not intentional about shaping your narrative, it will be shaped by others based on their own thoughts and opinions. Therefore you need to be proactive in crafting your brand and reputation so you don't leave it up to chance. This is a lesson we've seen played out many times, and we have interviewed multiple experts who have validated this point.

Sometimes, that shaping happens in ways that can make or break your career trajectory.

FROM ANALYST TO COO: A LESSON IN EXECUTIVE PRESENCE

Sometimes this happens in subtle, but important, ways that can significantly impact your career trajectory. May Busch learned this lesson firsthand during her impressive 24-year career at Morgan Stanley, where she rose from junior analyst to become Chief Operating Officer for Europe. The path wasn't always smooth.

May, who had built a reputation as a hardworking professional climbing the ranks through good judgment and long hours, was working late one evening on the trading floor when her boss approached her. What he said impacted the course of her career more than one might expect: he recommended a fashion designer.

At first, May thought he was talking about a personal shopper. Her boss then walked her around the trading floor, asking every woman still there at 7:30 PM if they knew who Jil Sander was. They all did. Jil Sander was the "it" fashion designer for women's power suits at the time.

The trouble was that, despite her capabilities, May wasn't projecting the executive presence expected at senior levels. "I was getting mistaken for flight attendants in airports," May recalls. "I think one outfit even had a little bow." Despite her great work and dedication to the job, she wasn't being seen as someone who *belonged* in the senior ranks. When promotion time came around, she didn't get one.

Looking back, May realized what had likely happened in those behind-closed-doors promotion meetings. Her boss would have advocated for her, saying "What about Busch?" And the response would have been, "You mean that person who looks like a junior analyst?"

The wake-up call was surely unpleasant, but May's response demonstrates the strategic mindset that would eventually make her a C-suite executive. Rather than taking it personally or getting defensive, she focused on her goal: advancement. "If that's what's missing," she thought, "that's so easily remedied." She invested in a professional wardrobe that matched the identity of the role she wanted, not the role she currently held. "Dress for the job you want," right?

And while the clothes you wear are only a small part of your image, we also heard a similar story in a recent conversation with Ashan Willy, CEO of New Relic, a San Francisco tech company with over 2,000 employees. He said that when he was about to take on his first CEO role, the biggest piece of feedback and advice he got from the outgoing CEO was that he needed to upgrade his wardrobe and "dress better" so people took him more seriously.

These stories illustrate an important truth about personal branding: while competence and results are at the core of your career, how you present yourself matters in how others perceive your potential. You have to pair excellence in your work with strategic self-presentation. Why not take the one additional step to ensure your external presentation doesn't create unnecessary barriers to recognition of your capabilities? May's willingness to adapt this aspect of her brand, combined with her continued excellence, ultimately contributed to her rise to one of the most senior roles in global finance.

MAKE YOUR VALUE KNOWN OR RISK BEING OVERLOOKED

Shaping the narrative of how you want to be known has a lot of practical applications. Maybe your parents advised you to just "put your head down and work hard" and that quality work would speak for itself, but you've noticed that certain people tend to get rewarded more simply because they're more vocal about their work and accomplishments.

Gemma Stow, a UK-based self-promotion and visibility expert for female executives, shared with us on a podcast that, "performance only accounts for about ten percent of overall success in career progression. The rest comes from reputation, exposure, brand, and network, among other things—that's where self-promotion comes in."

Obviously, you don't want to be constantly bragging or promoting yourself. But strategic visibility about your work and accomplishments is essential for career progression in today's modern working world.

Shaping your narrative has major implications in today's gig economy where short-term contracts, freelance work, and project-based roles are becoming more common than traditional, long-term employment. Andy wrote about this trend in *Own Your Career, Own Your Life*, and Mike's first book, *You Are the Brand*, became a *Wall Street Journal* bestseller largely because more professionals are pivoting toward freelancing and consulting. As more organizations embrace project-based work and encourage internal mobility, your reputation and visibility can determine whether you're tapped for that next promotion or invited onto a high-profile cross-functional project.

Many large companies are going as far as creating robust talent marketplaces where employees can register their skills, experience, certifications, and development plans and then get matched to different roles or be given guidance on how to reach certain roles down the road.

While these platforms are a great resource and may help companies identify the right employees for different roles, building a strong career that you love (and truly owning your career), will require employees to be proactive in taking advantage of these resources and even pitching themselves for internal roles.

We acknowledge that there is still a lot of unconscious bias out there for hiring and project decisions. Progress has been made, but unfortunately some people still take gender, race, religion, age, and other things into consideration (even when they don't think they are doing it). If you come from an underrepresented group, then, building a personal brand can be even more important.

When Andy interviewed his friend, Kay Fabella, a sought-after DEI consultant, for his first book, she told him that if you are in a traditionally overlooked group, you need to proactively increase your visibility and be even more proactive in building your brand. Kay says, "When you are an 'only' in the room, you have to work even harder to step up, speak up, and advocate for yourself. If your potential employer or your future colleagues don't know what your experience is or what skills you bring to the table, nothing will change for you—or for the people from your community who come after you."

Kay continues, "As an individual from an underrepresented group, you have an even greater responsibility to your community to share your story, put your expertise out there consistently, and make yourself more visible to pave the way for others. Because change can only happen when the 'only's' become one of many. Stepping up and showing up is how minorities can take a seat at the table and reshape the conversation."

These conversations about visibility and narrative play out in very practical ways. While face-to-face interactions and workplace performance remain important, much of your narrative-shaping now happens in digital spaces where first impressions are formed before you ever meet someone in person.

Now, let's get practical about where most of this narrative-shaping happens today.

FROM CORPORATE EXECUTIVE TO BESTSELLING AUTHOR

Mita Mallick was a corporate executive in charge of inclusion and multicultural marketing at a large multinational corporation when she started sharing thoughts online, including the good and bad experiences she had in the corporate world, as a way to raise awareness about problems and help others. Her message resonated deeply with people and her follower count grew considerably. Today she's a *Wall Street Journal* bestselling author of two books and workplace strategist with nearly 200,000 followers on LinkedIn.

When we asked her for her take on personal branding, she told us, "job security is dead. We have to all be prepared that tomorrow, our company may show us the door. Building your personal brand is key to staying relevant in this marketplace. An authentic and memorable personal brand is also what will help you connect with more individuals, attract new opportunities, and open doors to different career pathways that you hadn't considered before."

This has certainly paid off for Mita, who has become a top voice on LinkedIn, started an award-winning pod-

SHAPE YOUR NARRATIVE OR SOMEONE ELSE WILL

cast, published two books, joined advisory boards, been on small and large public stages, and so much more.

And while you may not want all of those things, Mita says, "don't underestimate the power of developing your personal brand. It can be a game changer."

THE WEB IS YOUR CV

One obvious place to shape your narrative is online. As of this writing, Vala Afshar serves as the Chief Digital Evangelist for Salesforce. With a following of over one million on X and LinkedIn, Afshar is a prominent voice in the business and technology sectors.

He says, "The traditional resume is dead. The web is your CV, and your personal brand is your digital footprint plus your digital exhaust." Afshar certainly practices what he preaches: he contributes weekly articles to ZDNet, has written over 600 articles for major media outlets, and hosts a popular weekly video podcast, DisrupTV, which regularly gets more than 100,000 views per episode.

Afshar likens your digital presence to the exhaust from a car, a continuous trail that follows you everywhere you go online. This trail is all your social media posts, online interactions, and any digital content you create, and it's an important part of your personal brand.

Social media is important for internal mobility, too; for people already working at large organizations, LinkedIn can function as a CV for internal mobility.

The numbers back this up. Recent surveys state:

- 82% of Americans agree companies are more influential if their executives have a personal brand they know and follow (PR News wire)

- 67% of all Americans would be willing to spend more money on products and services from companies of founders whose personal brand aligns with their own values (Brand Builders Group)

- 80% of marketing executives say they are actively developing their own personal brand (CMO Council)

Personal branding relies on your past. Old social media posts, even from many years ago, can sometimes resurface and impact your professional reputation or job prospects. We don't always want the things we said in our teens or twenties to come back to us in our thirties or forties, do we?

To help with this, companies like LifeBrand use AI to scan your social media history and flag content that may no longer reflect your values or goals. Employers today care about intelligence and emotional awareness, but they're also paying attention to digital intelligence. This means understanding how you look online, and how others perceive your digital presence. Even something as small as typing in all capital letters can send the wrong message.

Every post, comment, and share contributes to your personal brand. You don't need to censor yourself, but you do need to keep this in mind. Ask yourself if what you share online supports the reputation you want to build.

And many company CEOs are starting to see how this benefits not only their brand, but also their organization's brand, which we'll discuss more in Chapter 9. One example is Hal Lawton, the CEO of Tractor Supply Company, who shares regular updates on LinkedIn, where he has 46,000+ followers as of this writing.

Knowing what you want to be known for starts with seeing your past work through a different lens. When you look beyond your job titles and responsibilities, you may start to see patterns in how you think, lead, or contribute. These patterns reveal the brand you have today and help you define the one you want to build.

Unfortunately, most of us are unaware of our own expertise. Let's walk through a few simple exercises to help you uncover that.

HOW TO IDENTIFY YOUR UNIQUE EXPERTISE

Many of our clients have found the following exercise extremely helpful. All of us have roles and responsibilities as outlined in our job description, but there are many other secondary things we do that often go unnoticed, even by ourselves. This is often where we see some of our softer skills come to light.

We shared a bit of our own journeys in the previous chapter, but let's take a bird's eye view as to how this can all come together. When Mike was in his mid-twenties, he worked at an after-school academy preparing high school kids for their college entrance exams. Then in his 30s he took the role of music director at a church. It may seem like all he was responsible for was to teach classes or put on a good music program, but there are tons of other things that go with those roles.

For the after-school academy, students had to be encouraged, heard, and helped one-on-one. He had to meet with parents to help them help their children. He had to promote some of the programs the academy offered, and facilitate meetings with other teachers. For the music role, he had to recruit volunteers, market albums they recorded, and plan and host conferences. None of this was on his job descriptions, but they were all important parts of his roles.

When Mike listed out these responsibilities, here's how they looked:

1. I taught high school students.
2. I counseled students on their grades.
3. I wrote curriculums.
4. I recruited music team volunteers.
5. I marketed the albums we recorded.
6. I hosted conferences for the church.

If you simply cross out the end of each of those sentences, you may start seeing yourself in a new light:

1. I taught ~~high school students~~.
2. I counseled ~~students on their grades~~.
3. I wrote ~~curriculums~~.

4. I recruited ~~music team volunteers~~.
5. I marketed ~~the albums we recorded~~.
6. I hosted conferences ~~for the church~~.

For Andy, it looked something like this:

1. I coached youth sports
2. I analyzed data
3. I facilitated workshops
4. I wrote papers
5. I spoke in meetings
6. I hosted happy hours and events

Crossing off the lines ends up looking something like this:

1. I coached ~~youth sports~~
2. I analyzed ~~data~~
3. I facilitated ~~workshops~~
4. I wrote ~~papers~~
5. I spoke ~~in meetings~~
6. I hosted ~~happy hours and events~~

For so much of our lives, we see ourselves through the lens of a company, organization, or role rather than the skills we possess or who we inherently are. We fail to see our unique expertise. Seeing those words on the page can shift your mindset and even become mantras: "I am a teacher! I am a counselor! I am a writer! I am a recruiter! I am a marketer! I am a conference host!"

THE "I AM" EXERCISE

Now, let's try to expand to how you see yourself as a complete person. This foundational exercise helps you identify all the facets of your identity, both professional and personal, so you can understand the complete picture of who you are beyond your work capabilities.

Take out a journal or piece of paper and write "I am..." at the top. Below that, list all the nouns and adjectives you identify with. Don't overthink this. Include current realities, roles you play, characteristics you possess, and even aspirational elements.

Your list might include professional roles (manager, consultant, teacher), personal identities (parent, partner, friend), characteristics (creative, analytical, empathetic), interests (runner, reader, traveler), values (honest, reliable, curious), and life experiences that have shaped you (cancer survivor, immigrant, first-generation college graduate).

And remember that you don't have to be "world class" to include something. For example, if you keep a regular journal and enjoy writing, you might consider yourself a writer, even if you've never published anything.

For example, Andy's list includes:

- Author
- Keynote speaker
- Facilitator
- Podcaster
- Content creator

- Conference and community host
- Connector
- Husband
- Father
- Brother
- Son
- Friend
- Dog owner
- Cyclist
- Outdoors enthusiast
- Expat
- Self-confident
- Adventurous
- A world traveler
- Growth-minded
- Health conscious
- An athlete
- Healthy
- Cancer free
- A lifelong learner

Mike's list might include:

- Personal branding expert
- Author
- Speaker
- Entrepreneur
- Teacher
- Korean-American

- Creative
- Storyteller
- Brother
- Son
- Music lover
- Community builder
- Mentor
- Strategic thinker
- Problem solver

After you complete your list, circle the three to five items that feel most central to who you are. These might be the identities that, if taken away, would fundamentally change how you see yourself. These core identities should influence how you think about your personal brand and career direction.

When you can clearly articulate who you are in all your complexity, you're better equipped to make authentic choices about your career, relationships, and life direction. Most importantly, you'll start to see that your personal brand isn't something you need to create from scratch. It's already there, woven into who you are and how you naturally show up in the world. You start recognizing, owning, and strategically expressing the identity you already possess.

And you can use these identifications and characteristics to start to define the brand you want to have as well as where you want to go in your career. You can also look and see what might be missing for your brand or future career goals.

Reinventing yourself is just as much about changing the story you tell yourself as it is changing the story you tell the public. It's as if you are rebranding yourself *to yourself*. Perhaps you feel torn between the life you live vs. the life yet-to-be-lived, or feel weighed down by second-guessing, self-doubt, and frustration.

This is normal, friend. But if you're going to be your own worst critic, you also have to learn how to be your own biggest fan. Our hope is that these simple exercises help you see yourself in a new light.

SHAPING YOUR NARRATIVE TO OTHERS

You've now completed two foundational exercises for narrative-shaping. First, you identified your unique expertise by recognizing all the skills you've developed through your work experience, often capabilities you didn't even realize you possessed. Second, you explored your complete identity through the "I Am" exercise, seeing yourself as a whole person beyond just your professional roles.

Now we reach the third step: examining how others currently perceive you and how you want to be known moving forward. This bridges your internal self-awareness with your external reputation.

When shaping your narrative, you need to work on both sides of the equation: how you see yourself and how others see you, as these two aspects are closely linked. Your internal narrative influences how you show up, and how you show up influences others' perceptions of you. The reflection questions below help you identify any gaps between your authentic identity and your external reputation.

1. What do I want to be known for, and what am I currently known for?

2. If someone introduced me in a meeting or at a networking event, what would I want them to say?

3. What do colleagues or clients often thank me or admire me for?

4. When I talk about my work, do I lead with skills, impact, or titles?

5. What is one story or example I could share that reflects the kind of work or person I want to be known for?

Remember, shaping your narrative is all about positioning yourself to act on the opportunities that perception creates. Once you're clear on who you are and how you want to be known, the next step is learning how to lead and create impact regardless of your current title or position in the organizational chart.

Let's put this chapter into action, either with a notebook or our free workbook.

1. Complete the **Identifying Your Unique Expertise** exercise. List all the tasks and responsibilities from your previous jobs. Then, remove the job-specific context to help reveal your core skills.

2. Complete the **"I Am" Exercise**. Create your comprehensive identity list, then circle the 3-5 items that feel most central to who you are. Identify which items feel aspirational and could guide your professional development.

3. What do your past experiences reveal about your natural strengths, values, and ways of working regardless of industry?

4. Answer the **Shaping Your Narrative** questions so you can identify any gaps between your intention and your perception. You begin to find true alignment with yourself when you define how you want to be known, and start reinforcing that in both your inner and outer voice.

5. Review your social media and professional profiles. Identify posts or content that reinforce your current or past career. Are there any posts you can re-purpose? Are there any posts you might consider archiving or deleting? If so, archive or delete them, or at least try to commit to pause on posting content like that for the time being. You don't want to get yourself in trouble.

CHAPTER FOUR:

INTRAPRENEURSHIP: HOW TO LEAD WITHOUT A TITLE

The debate over the greatest NBA players of all time is one of the most heated in sports. Who's the best—Jordan? LeBron? Kobe? Wilt? These discussions can be fun, but superstars alone don't win championships.

Every great team needs players who know their role and execute at a high level. You'll often hear about players who bring veteran presence to a locker room, set the defensive tone, or bring chemistry that holds the team together. These players don't always get the headlines, but their leadership can matter just as much. Some of the greatest superstars in history openly credit their teams' success to these players.

In fact, many of today's superstars actually developed within established systems before becoming household names. Think about players like Kawhi Leonard, who was drafted 15th overall and developed his skills within the San Antonio Spurs' championship culture before moving on elsewhere. Or Draymond Green, a second-round pick who became the defensive anchor and emotional leader of the Golden State Warriors dynasty. While they didn't arrive as superstars, these players earned their stripes by mastering their roles, studying the game, and consistently finding ways to add value beyond what was expected.

The same dynamic exists in the corporate world. Leadership isn't limited to the person with the biggest title. Unlike a basketball team that can only have five players on the court, organizations have room for countless people to step up, take ownership, and lead from wherever they are.

In the last chapter, we explored shaping your narrative through the stories you tell and actions you take. But shaping your narrative isn't just about external storytelling; it also happens in your day-to-day work. Sometimes the most important change happens right where you are: stepping up, solving problems, and leading without waiting for a title. That's the heart of *intrapreneurship*.

Intrapreneurship is taking ownership and initiative inside an established organization. Like entrepreneurs, intrapreneurs solve problems, think creatively, and drive change, but they do it within the structure of a company. Many professionals wait until they're given tasks or authority. Intrapreneurs create the very opportunities others are still waiting for.

Think about how different work feels today compared to just five years ago. Your team is probably scattered across different time zones, half your meetings happen over video calls, and the pace of change seems to accelerate every quarter. This new reality has created massive gaps that only certain types of people know how to fill.

The speed of business today means companies can't wait for the next planning cycle to address problems. They need people who can move quickly, think on their feet, and execute without needing their hand held. While some employees are waiting for permission or clearer instructions, intrapreneurs are already steps ahead, testing solutions and making progress. They create value that's impossible to ignore.

In her book, *Impact Players*, researcher and bestselling author Liz Wiseman asserts that the most valuable employees in organizations are those who do not let their title or role limit them and instead proactively look for ways to add value to their team and organization. We call this being an intrapreneur.

So what does this look like in practice? Let's look at a few everyday examples of intrapreneurship at work.

***

Before stepping out to build her own consultancy, Ellin Sidell held a leadership role at Costco. She wasn't hired to drive organizational change but she saw a clear problem: employees craved mentorship, but the existing program could only accommodate a small number of people. Year after year, Costco had to turn away dozens of employees who wanted to grow and develop.

Instead of just flagging the issue to leadership, Ellin proposed a new model: mentorship circles, where groups of mentees could learn from mentors in a scalable format. She had experience with mentorship circles from Microsoft, where she once lobbied to become a co-mentor in a similar program.

The structure made sense. With a group format, one mentor could guide multiple mentees at once, scaling the impact. Mentees could also learn from each other, creating an ecosystem of shared knowledge and networking opportunities.

Ellin spent months advocating for the program internally, refining the model, and seeking support from key stakeholders. The result was seventeen mentees, split into two rings. Word spread, and more employees wanted in. Within a short time, the program had proven itself and become an integral part of leadership development within the company.

Ellin also unlocked another benefit: building strong relationships with senior leaders. She expanded her network beyond her immediate team, forming relationships with influential leaders who saw her initiative firsthand.

Not all intrapreneurship looks like Ellin's structured approach. Sometimes it requires getting creative when traditional methods fail.

Henry Jeong, a recruiter in New York City, was given a mission-critical assignment: find a foreman with a specific, specialized, and rare boiler certification. A foreman with this particular certification had to be on-site at all times, otherwise the facility would be forced to shut down.

The challenge was that this type of candidate was nearly impossible to find via traditional recruiting methods. These professionals didn't spend time on LinkedIn, and they weren't actively applying for jobs. Regular boolean searches, job postings, and typical outreach strategies led nowhere.

Henry had to think outside of the box, so he asked a different question: "If these people weren't online, where would they be?"

He realized they would need to purchase parts to do their jobs, which meant they would likely visit parts stores. Henry took the unconventional step of asking a local parts store to let him set up a small table near the entrance with a sign saying he was looking for a foreman with the specialized certification. A few days later, he found the right candidate at the parts store and hired him.

Pretty smart solution, if you ask us! Henry's company was equally impressed, and his approach earned attention. Leadership began to rely on him for difficult and urgent placements, and Henry became known for being resourceful, action-oriented, and deeply committed to results.

The way you solve problems, advocate for change, and lead without a title sends a powerful message about who you are and what you're capable of.

Instead of seeing your job through a narrow lens, look at it from the perspective of your manager or your organization as a whole. What are the broader goals? What challenges are blocking progress? The more you understand what matters to the business, the easier it becomes to spot opportunities where you can contribute. Sometimes intrapreneurship leads to huge career change.

FROM VIDEO ROOM TO NBA CHAMPIONSHIP COACH: THE ERIK SPOELSTRA STORY

In 1995, Erik Spoelstra was organizing game footage as the Miami Heat's video coordinator. Today, he's one of the NBA's most successful and highest-paid coaches.

How did he make that leap? His video position might sound unglamorous, but Spoelstra approached it like an intrapreneur. Instead of simply cataloging plays and preparing footage, Spoelstra analyzed patterns, identified trends, and began offering insights from his unique vantage point. He studied what happened on the court and why. He noticed which defensive schemes worked against specific offensive sets. He tracked shooting percentages from different court positions. He became a student of basketball analytics before analytics were even trendy.

When assistant coaches were preparing for upcoming opponents, Spoelstra would proactively share observations that could help with game planning. When players were struggling with specific aspects of their game, he'd compile footage that could help them improve. He turned a behind-the-scenes role into a strategic position.

Pat Riley, the Heat's president, later said that Spoelstra's hunger to learn and contribute was unlike anything he'd seen. In 2008, when Riley stepped down as head coach, he hand-picked Spoelstra as his successor.

The results speak for themselves: since he took over, Spoelstra has led the Heat to six NBA Finals appearances, winning championships in 2012 and 2013. Perhaps the most remarkable part of Spoelstra's journey is this: he's spent his entire professional career with one organization. He built his career by consistently asking, "How can I add more value *right where I am?*"

You don't need to stay with one organization for your entire career—it is, we admit, a little extreme for most people these days—but Spoelstra's story shows where intrapreneurship can lead within your current organization.

Sometimes it can transform entire industries, as we'll see in this next section.

KEN KUTARAGI AND THE BIRTH OF PLAYSTATION

In 1975, Ken Kutaragi was a 25-year-old electrical engineer working in Sony's sound labs. He wasn't part of Sony's strategic planning team, and he certainly wasn't supposed to be thinking about video games. At the time, Sony had zero interest in gaming. Executives viewed it as nothing more than a toy industry.

But Kutaragi saw something different when he bought his young daughter a Nintendo Famicom console. As he watched her play, he became frustrated with the poor sound quality. His engineering background told him that a dedicated digital sound chip could dramatically improve the gaming experience—or, at least, the gaming experience's audio.

Most employees would have just accepted the limitation and moved on, but Kutaragi did something that almost got him fired: he began working as a consultant for Nintendo, developing the very sound chip he envisioned.

When Sony's senior executives discovered his side project, they were furious. Fortunately for Kutaragi—and for Sony's future—CEO Norio Ohga saw potential where others had only seen insubordination. Instead of firing him, Ohga encouraged the project and allowed Kutaragi to work with Nintendo on developing a CD-ROM-based gaming system they called the "Play Station."

But then Nintendo decided to abandon the partnership and go in a different direction. Kutaragi saw an opportunity and approached Sony's leadership with a bold proposition: if Nintendo didn't want the gaming technology, why shouldn't Sony enter the gaming business themselves?

Most of Sony's senior management remained skeptical, and still saw gaming as beneath Sony's brand. But Kutaragi persisted, and CEO Ohga backed the development of Sony's own gaming console.

The eventual result was the PlayStation, which launched in Japan in December 1994. It became the first gaming console to ship over 100 million units in under a decade. By 1998, the PlayStation was generating 40% of Sony Corporation's operating profits. Eventually, Kutaragi was promoted to Chairman and CEO of Sony Computer Entertainment, the newly created gaming division. Under his leadership, Sony went on to launch the PlayStation 2 and PlayStation 3, selling over 525 million PlayStation units by 2018.

What started as one engineer's frustration with his daughter's gaming experience became a multi-billion-dollar business unit that changed Sony's entire corporate strategy. Kutaragi's story is a strong lesson in intrapreneurship: sometimes the biggest opportunities come from industries your company isn't even considering.

***

The difference between people who naturally step into intrapreneurial roles and those who don't often come down to how they think about their work. Most of us have invisible mental boundaries that we don't even realize are there—lines we've drawn around what's "our job" and what isn't, what we're "allowed" to do and what we're not.

The biggest shift is probably the most obvious one: moving from "That's not my job" to "How can I help?"

That said, we're not suggesting you become the office pushover who takes on everyone else's work. But there's something important about starting to look for ways to solve problems and add value regardless of your title or job description. When you see something that's clearly not working well, instead of thinking "Well, that's too bad, but it's not my problem," you might wonder instead, "What would happen if I actually tried to fix this?" Most of the time, a manager or colleague will appreciate genuine offers to make things better, especially when you're clear that you're trying to add value and not take over or muscle anybody out.

Another thing that holds people back is waiting for the perfect moment or the perfect solution. A good intrapreneur probably knows that good enough, implemented today, beats perfect, delivered never. They're comfortable with trying something, seeing how it works, and improving it along the way.

Maybe most importantly, they've learned to zoom out from their immediate responsibilities and think about the bigger picture. They start paying attention to what their manager is trying to accomplish, what challenges their department is facing, and where the company is trying to go. That broader perspective helps them spot opportunities that others miss and position their ideas in ways that actually get support.

PRACTICAL WAYS TO STEP INTO INTRAPRENEURSHIP

These are great stories, but they all started small. You don't need a big initiative or groundbreaking idea to begin showing up as an intrapreneur. Here are some ideas:

1. Spot and Solve a Small Problem

Maybe you can look around your team or department and identify a recurring frustration or inefficiency. Is there a process everyone complains about, but no one has improved? Are people wasting time looking for files, redoing work, or waiting for approvals?

If there's anything like this, try to think of a way to improve it and write it down, then share it with your manager or a trusted teammate. It doesn't need to be perfect; it just needs to be useful.

2. Create a Playbook for a Repeatable Task

If you find yourself doing the same task multiple times or training others on it, write the process down. What are the steps? What are the pitfalls to avoid? Where do people usually get stuck?

You can make that knowledge into a short how-to manual and share it with your team. It might help you become known as someone who makes things easier and more efficient.

3. Anticipate Your Manager's Needs

Ask yourself (or your manager directly), "What's one thing my manager is trying to accomplish this quarter? How can I help make that happen more effectively or smoothly?"

Can you gather information, draft something, or remove a bottleneck? Can you do something that will make their job easier? Even being able to help a little bit would show initiative and build trust.

4. Look for Cross-Department Gaps

Are there places where communication between teams breaks down, and if so, could you be a kind of bridge? You could volunteer to sit in on a meeting with another team, or offer to document a shared process that gets lost in translation. Something like suggesting a shared doc or Slack channel can go a long way.

5. Document and Share What Works

You don't always need a new idea; sometimes it's about spreading what's already working. Did you find a shortcut to onboard new team members faster? Did your presentation format help clarify a complex project? Can you create a new standard operating procedure to make things more efficient in the future? It's good to think about things like these.

Package what worked and share it internally as a resource. You'll start to build a reputation as someone who makes things better and easier for others.

A lot of professionals spend a lot of time waiting: waiting for permission, waiting for a promotion, waiting for someone else to validate their potential. The people who rise are the ones who lead before they're asked to. Every great company is built on people who manage both to do their jobs and redefine them.

Remember how we opened this chapter: great teams don't just win because of a superstar, but because other players step up and lead in not insignificant ways.

Intrapreneurship is how you become that kind of teammate. You can shape the culture, raise the standard, and make the whole team better simply by being there like someone who cares enough to make things better.

And in becoming an intrapreneur, you'll also boost your personal brand as someone who is valuable to the team and the organization.

Ready to put all of this into practice? Here are some exercises to get you started. As always, you can find the complete workbook with additional resources at ownyourbrandbook.com. Look around your current role and organization to identify where you can make an impact:

1. **Where do you hear recurring complaints or frustration at work?**

   List one specific problem that comes up often but no one has addressed. What might a small first step toward solving it look like?

2. **What skill or knowledge do you have that could help another team—even if it's not part of your job description?**

   How might you offer that help? Who would benefit?

3. **What's one thing your manager or team is trying to accomplish this quarter?**

Ask yourself: How could I contribute meaningfully to that goal beyond my normal role, even if indirectly?

4. **Where do you notice communication breaking down across departments or roles?**

What would it look like to bridge that gap, or make it easier for others to collaborate?

5. **What task or process do you repeat often that others could learn from?**

Write it out or record it with a screen recorder like Loom. Could it become a shared resource or simple playbook? There is a good chance that you do some things that others would like to learn from.

THINK LIKE AN INTRAPRENEUR

These questions help shift your mindset from "That's not my job" to "How can I add value?"

- Where are you waiting for permission, rather than taking initiative?

- What's one idea you've had recently but kept to yourself?

- If you zoomed out and looked at your role through your manager's eyes, what would stand out as a missed opportunity?

- What would you do to create more value for the organization or team if you were not waiting for a request or permission?

- What is something you could do that would make your boss or client's job easier?

We haven't yet discussed AI much, but there are many tools you could use to help you with these questions and exercises and give you ideas for how to provide more value to your boss, team, or clients. And speaking of AI...

Coming up next: As AI changes the workplace at unprecedented speed, more than a few people are worried about being replaced. But in the next chapter, we'll explore the seven deeply-human traits that we believe will become even more valuable in an AI-driven world—these are traits that no algorithm can replicate, and that will set your personal brand apart.

CHAPTER FIVE:
SEVEN HUMAN TRAITS THAT WILL MATTER EVEN MORE IN THE AGE OF AI

As we write this book, the world of work is changing at breakneck speed. Artificial intelligence is already reshaping what we do, how we do it, and what careers will look like tomorrow. AI can write emails, summarize meetings, analyze data, and even generate creative ideas. Tasks that once took entire teams can now be done with a single prompt—at least, as long as it's written well enough.

That shift may terrify anyone coasting in their career. But for those who are curious, creative, and driven, we believe this shift is an open door.

While no one can predict the future with absolute certainty, a few trends are clear. Work is becoming more collaborative; AI can complete individual tasks faster than ever, but humans are still the ones who will align strategy, manage stakeholders, and navigate personalities.

Trust continues to drive decision-making, and if anything, it will become even more important because people will sift past AI content to get to the human parts of business—whether pitching an idea, leading a team, or closing a deal. As more routine work becomes commoditized, the ability to make tough calls, communicate with an increasingly diverse workforce, and read between the lines will also gain new value.

In this chapter, we'll explore seven human traits that we believe will set you apart and elevate your personal brand as well as your career, even when everyone has access to the same AI tools.

1. EMOTIONAL INTELLIGENCE (EQ): CAN YOU READ YOURSELF BEFORE READING THE ROOM?

We've all worked with that one person who steamrolled teammates, dismissed feedback, or created drama wherever they went. Maybe they hit their numbers, led major projects, or had sharp ideas, but over time it became clear that their presence cost more than it contributed. If they happened to leave or were let go, everyone else seemed to breathe a little easier.

This person isn't necessarily low-intelligence, but they're probably low on *emotional intelligence*. Emotional intelligence, or EQ, is the ability to recognize, understand, and manage emotions, both your own and those of others. People with high EQ are generally more self-aware and curious. They ask thoughtful questions, resolve conflict without creating collateral damage, and lead with empathy.

We're not counselors or therapists, but we've both tried to incorporate into our lives a few simple practices that can help anyone grow in emotional intelligence. One of the most effective is journaling.

Most of us move through life in patterns we don't fully notice. When you regularly write down what you're experiencing, feeling, or grateful for, you begin to spot those patterns and gain perspective on what's actually happening beneath the surface.

One place to start is by thinking about your emotions and perceptions of others and regularly asking yourself why you feel a certain way. For example, when a coworker sends a poorly-worded email or ignores something you said or did, what did you feel and why? Did they break an unwritten rule you had but didn't communicate? Have you considered their perspective and have you given them feedback to help them improve?

Another great thing you can do is to start keeping a gratitude journal. Every morning, try to write three things you're grateful for. They don't have to be big, and in fact, the smaller and more specific, the better: a great cup of coffee, the opportunity to lead a meeting, even the weather.

This helps rewire your brain to notice what's good in your life, even when life is hard or chaotic.

As psychologist and gratitude researcher Dr. Robert Emmons says, "Gratitude blocks toxic emotions, such as envy, resentment, regret, and depression, which can destroy our happiness."

Emmons' research has shown that people who keep gratitude journals report fewer negative physical symptoms, feel better about their lives, sleep more soundly, and are more optimistic about the future. From a workplace perspective, they're also more resilient, more collaborative, and better at handling stress.

Practicing gratitude makes you more grounded and a better colleague, manager, and leader. We've all been around people who carry a sense of calm, warmth, and humility. Odds are they've practiced emotional regulation in some way, and have learned to move through life with a deeper sense of appreciation for it.

We have both experienced this for ourselves. When Andy was diagnosed with testicular cancer and going through treatment in early 2021, he persisted with his gratitude practice and wrote down at least three things every single day, even on the hardest days, and found that it really helped him get through the hard times.

And while you may not be going through a major health crisis like cancer (we hope), we have found work situations can be almost as stressful. So when your co-worker ignores you or your boss gives you extra work you don't want to do, you are certainly allowed to be frustrated. But you can also write down how grateful you are to have the job and paycheck to begin with as well as a family who loves you, or maybe your dog, or a good cup of coffee, or anything else you might be grateful for.

Try it for a week. Write three things you're grateful for and see if your lens starts to shift. The shift in attitude can also help you become more resilient as well, which will become more valuable in the future.

The expectation for healthy, self-aware, high-EQ people in the workforce is going to rise. The more aware you become of your own patterns and the more attuned you are to others, the more trust, clear understanding, and influence you will bring into every room.

2. JUDGMENT AND CRITICAL THINKING: DO YOU MAKE MOVES OR JUST TAKE ORDERS?

The World Economic Forum's 2025 Future of Jobs Report lists "analytical thinking" as the number one core skill in demand. That may surprise some, in the face of how good AI has become at analyzing information. We believe that's because sound judgment is becoming more rare. While AI can recommend what's probable, only humans can decide what's wise.

Analytical thinking is about breaking things down: examining data, spotting patterns, understanding cause and effect. It's methodical and detail-oriented. We still need people who can read the room, integrate perspectives, and ask hard questions that software and algorithms miss.

Closely related to analytical thinking is critical thinking, which is a broader skill that includes the ability to zoom out, weigh competing interests, and make reasoned decisions—especially when no option is perfect.

One of the best ways to sharpen your thinking is to study how top performers operate outside your own field. When you borrow mental models from disciplines like sports, psychology, or the arts, you expand your perspective and can learn how to make better decisions under pressure.

One person we've learned from is Lauren Johnson (laurenjohnsonandco.com), a mental performance coach who's worked with elite athletes on the New York Yankees and the U.S. Women's World Cup team. Today, she helps leaders and organizations build the mindset to perform consistently under stress.

Lauren's clients are some of the most talented athletes in the world. They have access to best-in-class training, data, and support. But in baseball, even the best hitters fail 70% of the time: a .300 batting average is elite.

This simple statistic can reframe how we think about failure in other parts of life. School trains us to see success as a percentage: get 90% of the answers right and you're elite. But high performance in life doesn't always work that way. If you apply to ten jobs and get three interviews, that could also be seen as a solid batting average rather than failure.

Top performers aren't perfect. What separates them from others is how they respond when things don't go their way. Lauren teaches that before elite athletes move on from mistakes, they pause, reflect, and recalibrate themselves. They ask better questions, evaluate their thinking, and train their decision-making like a skill.

That's a mindset worth adopting. Sometimes, you will

make the wrong call. A presentation will flop, a project won't land, and timing will be off. More than trying to avoid setbacks like these, the goal is to learn from them so that you can improve.

Watch how top performers operate in fields you're passionate about—even if they have nothing to do with your job. Whether it's pro athletes, chess grandmasters, master chefs, elite rock climbers, jazz musicians, or even competitive gamers, you'll see a throughline: mindset, consistency, and high standards under pressure.

These high performers train how they think. They make decisions fast, course-correct often, and stay curious even when they're at the top.

The same applies in your career. If you want to be seen as someone with good judgment, develop discernment. Treat your decision-making like a skill you're always upgrading.

3. STORYTELLING: CAN YOU SAY SOMETHING THAT STICKS?

Long before we had data, we had stories. Even in an AI-powered world, people still connect through stories. As Nobel Prize–winning psychologist Daniel Kahneman writes in his seminal book *Thinking, Fast and Slow*: "No one ever made a decision because of a number. They need a story."

Stories help us make sense of complex information, create emotional connections, and remember what's important. When we hear or read a good story, our brains release oxytocin, the "trust hormone," which creates connection with the story characters. This neurological response explains why stories are more persuasive than facts alone.

Stories also create meaning by shaping random events into coherent experiences with cause and effect. This is why ancient cultures used myths to explain natural phenomena, and why we still use stories today to make sense of our careers, relationships, and world events.

Your ability to communicate through story can set you apart in nearly any role. One way to sharpen your storytelling instinct is to start noticing what stories stick with you and why.

Think about your favorite movies, shows, or books. What moved you or made you angry? What endings felt earned, and which ones disappointed you? Those reactions will give you some idea. (And don't get us started on the final season of Game of Thrones).

The more you develop an eye for story, the more you'll see it everywhere. For example, take the winter sport called curling. Most people don't follow it year-round, but during the Winter Olympics, millions of people can become emotionally invested in this niche sport. Why might that be?

Somehow, there's something interesting about watching people slide heavy granite stones across ice while teammates furiously sweep in front of it to control the stone's path. But what transforms curling from a specialized sport into compelling human drama is story. On a broadcast, the announcers will take the time to explain the player's background, where they're from, and how they've performed in the past. Context like this creates a kind of narrative tension that gives us someone to root for and helps us understand the stakes. Without this story, we're just watching rocks slide on ice.

We'll go further on storytelling techniques for content, career transitions, and personal branding in Chapter 7. For now, just remember that stories move people, and the better attuned you are to them, the more impactful you become.

While stories connect us, today's workplace requires you to collaborate effectively with people from vastly different backgrounds and perspectives.

4. COLLABORATION & INCLUSION: CAN YOU WORK WITH ANYONE, ANYWHERE?

As teams become more global, interdisciplinary, and remote, the ability to navigate differences in communication styles and cultural norms has become pretty important. It's easy to assume others think and work like we do, but they certainly do not. Some people are planners, while other people improvise more. Some process out loud and others process quietly. Some prefer directness while others value nuance.

Without awareness of these dynamics, even teams with the best intentions can have a hard time connecting. Technology can help us communicate across borders, but it can't account for the unspoken dynamics that shape human connection.

Earlier we mentioned that Mike traveled to Uganda on a humanitarian trip to work with an organization called the Ugandan Water Project. As a longtime donor, he was excited to visit and volunteered to help their team with marketing and fundraising materials while there.

While AI tools helped generate content quickly, something was off. His fast-paced, direct communication style wasn't going to land well in Uganda's more relational, understated culture. Even though English is fluently spoken in Uganda, the tone of his material lacked a certain cultural resonance.

The real breakthroughs came from sitting side by side with the local team, exchanging ideas, and shaping the messages together. Instead of leading with urgent calls-to-action, they created stories that tried to honor the dignity of the communities being served (and hopefully succeeded).

By collaborating across cultural gulfs, they were able to co-create something better than either side could on their own. We think this is the future of work—and it won't be hampered by the fact that many people work remotely.

Andy recently had a chance to interview Keith Ferrazzi, bestselling author of multiple books including *Never Eat Alone* and his latest, *Never Lead Alone*, who told him that proactivity and curiosity in collaboration, more than technical skills, are the key competencies that will make individuals valuable and relevant in the age of AI and ongoing workplace disruption. He emphasized that collaboration isn't just a nice-to-have, but the core of how high-performing teams, leaders, and organizations will thrive in the new world of work.

In the face of this, we think it's very important to seek ways to proactively build relationships and collaborate with others in our organization to create more success.

We should consider questions like:

- Whose perspective are we missing?

- How might someone with a different background see this?

- What assumptions are we making that might limit our thinking?

By being more collaborative and inclusive, you can become someone people trust to lead in complexity.

5. ADAPTABILITY: ARE YOU LIGHT ON YOUR FEET OR STUCK IN YOUR WAYS?

Adaptability is the ability to shift your mindset, approach, or skill set to stay effective, all while the ground shifts beneath you. In today's workplace, expertise can feel like it has an expiration date. The professionals who thrive aren't always the ones who know the most, but the ones most willing to learn.

More than corporate buzzwords, "upskilling" and "reskilling" reflect a reality where professionals must continually evolve to remain relevant. And we think most of us know this to be true. Constant change is a necessary thing.

Mike has seen this in his own work as a marketer. In the earlier days of his career, great long-form copywriting was how you got results, but then platforms like Instagram shrunk our attention spans, and suddenly captions mattered more than paragraphs. Then YouTube came along, where success meant designing thumbnails and pairing them with video titles that could catch our attention.

Every change was like learning the craft all over again: different platforms, different rules, but the same need to connect and convert.

Adaptability is the cost of staying in the game.

This pattern plays out across the rest of the corporate world, too. HR leaders manage hybrid workforces and build culture remotely, and finance teams analyze real-time dashboards instead of static quarterly reports.

The days of getting a college degree and working in that field for 40 years are over, unfortunately. The world of work is changing too quickly, and we have to keep learning and adapting.

This bears repeating: everyone is learning in motion. Everyone. You can't rely on your company to give you everything you need to grow. The pace of change is too fast. Even the best organizations can't keep up with all the new tools, ideas, and use-cases that emerge every week. There's no monopoly on how to use this stuff, and no one's coming to teach it all to you.

The edge now belongs to those who are adaptable, self-directed, self-taught, and self-aware.

We know that maybe you feel overworked and under-resourced, but that's what makes this a defining opportunity. Start with these habits:

- **Adopt a learning mindset.** Rather than defending what you already know or how you do things, ask, "What can I learn here?"

- **Test and experiment.** Try small changes, like a new tool, workflow, or communication habit, to build confidence if you're feeling uncertain.

- **Learn from new people.** Talk to colleagues in other departments or industries. Cross-pollination sparks growth.

6. RESILIENCE: HOW WELL CAN YOU BOUNCE BACK?

If adaptability is about adjusting to change, resilience is about recovering from it. Setbacks are okay, and a fact of life; markets can shift, relationships can end, health can fail, jobs can disappear. The real test is whether you can navigate these troubles with focus and bounce back with some kind of purpose.

Some people appear naturally resilient, but most of us build it, slowly and deliberately. Our mindset is the most important place to start from. In her book, *Mindset: The*

New Psychology of Success, Dr. Carol Dweck introduced the idea of a growth mindset: the belief that you can learn and improve from every situation—even failure.

With a growth mindset, you can see obstacles as data, and failures are just lessons to help us improve in the future. By adopting a growth mindset, we can more easily turn challenges into opportunities. There's no such thing as a wasted experience: this idea changed Andy's life.

For years, he avoided risk and played it safe. He stuck to familiar work, stayed inside his comfort zone, and held back as much as he could. But after reading *Mindset* in 2016, he realized he had grown up with a very fixed mindset, with a major fear of failure, and he avoided taking risks as a result.

Can you relate? As a result, he started doing things that scared him: launching a podcast, sharing more online, hosting events, changing careers, writing a book, and later moving his family to Spain.

None of it was easy, and not all of it worked out perfectly, but each experience built resilience: and then came an even more important challenge.

In 2020, Andy was diagnosed with cancer. He had surgery for it within weeks, and what followed was the typical grueling treatment: chemotherapy, then complications like pancreatitis and a complete overhaul of his lifestyle. He adopted a plant-based diet, meditated daily, and invested heavily in holistic approaches from vitamin infusions to gut health protocols. He also kept a journal and wrote down his gratitude daily, as we talked about earlier.

"I didn't choose cancer," Andy says, "but I could choose how to face it. I could choose to own my situation and make the best of it."

Andy's defining characteristic, to some extent, became resilience. He tried to focus on what he could control: his attitude and habits. The experience tested him on every level, but it also revealed an inner strength he hadn't known he had.

When Andy went through cancer, how he responded shaped his reputation. People saw someone who faced something difficult with courage and ownership.

Something important that Andy learned is that we all face challenges, and we can overcome them more easily by asking important questions. Questions like:

- What's *good* about this?

- What can I learn from it?

- What does this make possible?

- What's in my control, and what's not?

- How can I take ownership and make the best of this situation?

Reframing challenges can shift you from reacting to reflection—and eventually to progress.

An important part of growing in resilience is the importance of community. The people around you are *extremely* important, so try to surround yourself with those who lift you up, push you to grow, and help you see clearly when you're in the middle of something hard. Andy and I have both had to pivot careers, navigate personal loss, and start over after things didn't go as planned. Each time, our community was a big part of helping us move forward.

Resilience is a capacity you can build by repeated exposure to challenge and a reflection on how you respond. In seasons of uncertainty or change, it becomes one of the most valuable assets you have.

7. TASTE AND DISCERNMENT: THE DIFFERENCE BETWEEN NOISE AND ART

Taste is hard to define, but we think it's something like your creative ability to sense what's resonant, what's beautiful, and what works. More than personal preference, it's a kind of refined perception that blends intuition, lived experience, and cultural context. Taste is hard to teach, but you can feel it.

You see taste in someone whose wardrobe choices just seem to work; you can hear it when a songwriter leaves an empty space in a song instead of adding another lyric. You feel it when a filmmaker lingers on a specific shot, trusting the audience to understand what it means. It goes much, much further than this, but we'll leave it here—for simplicity's sake.

In the business world, taste isn't reserved for artists or creatives. You see it in the product manager who knows which feature to build next even though the data seems to say otherwise. It shows up in the marketer who chooses a three-word headline that manages to say more than a paragraph.

Let's use Rick Rubin as an example. He's one of the most iconic music producers of our time, known for his work with artists across wildly different genres. Despite that, he doesn't play an instrument or run a sound board.

Rubin's genius is in listening and knowing what *not* to do. He helps artists strip everything down until only the core of their music remains: the part that matters the most.

Think about what Rubin does that AI cannot: He sat with Johnny Cash thirty years ago and recognized the man's weathered voice needed minimal production. He heard a Red Hot Chili Peppers jam and knew which guitar riffs to keep and which to cut. He can listen to an artist's rough demo and sense the one line that will make people stop in their tracks.

AI can analyze thousands of hit songs and recommend chord progressions, among other various things; but it can't *feel* the moment when an artist discovers something true about themselves in the studio.

AI can generate content, design logos, write code, and even produce short films. But it doesn't have decades of intuition. It hasn't lived, failed, obsessed, or fallen in love with great work. It doesn't know why one image lingers in your mind and another doesn't.

But *you* do.

If you have that kind of eye, or want to develop it, you'll be even more valuable in the years ahead. We're happy to inform you that taste can be cultivated. You don't need to be born with it; you just need to practice it. Here's how:

- **Curate what you consume.** Your inputs shape your instincts. Follow creators, designers, filmmakers, thinkers, and even chefs whose work you admire. Be intentional about who fills your feed, because that's what fills your mind.

- **Pay attention to what resonates with you.** When something moves you, stop and ask why: was it the framing of the shot in the film? The meaningful way a character gave a certain speech? The brightness of the focal point in a photo? The immediacy of the imagery in a sentence (shoutout to Hemingway)? Just try to notice and think about why you like something. It sharpens your idea of what's good and what's not.

- **Edit your own life.** The way you dress, arrange your home, plan your day, write an email, or present a deck: these are all reflections of taste. Try to ask yourself: what feels cluttered? What feels clear? What feels like *me*?

- **Study great work.** Rewatch your favorite films with the director commentary on. Read the same paragraph three times and notice the rhythm of the language. You can increase your taste by trying to understand the decisions that led to a great work instead of just the end product.

- **Practice subtraction.** You can sometimes see evidence of taste by what's *not* present in something. A great design doesn't have too much. A powerful speech doesn't say *everything*. A good watercolor might be defined by what's not in the painting, as opposed to what is. So if you can, it's good to try to learn to say more with less.

- **Ask people whose taste you trust to critique your work.** Whether it's writing, design, presentations, or even your wardrobe, try to get feedback from those whose eye you respect. You'll see more clearly through theirs.

Taste is the practical skill of knowing what matters, with an artistic sensibility, and what to leave out. When others churn out AI-generated everything, your unique sense of what's "just right" can become a competitive edge.

As AI and technology do more and more of our work and make us more productive as a society, the most valuable traits of the future will be deeply human. Yes: you need to learn the tools, use the tech, and stay current. But don't outsource the parts of you that are uncopyable.

These seven traits—emotional intelligence, judgment, storytelling, collaboration, adaptability, resilience, and taste—are your insurance policy in an uncertain future.

The exercises below are designed to help you identify where you already show strength and where you can grow in the deeply human skills that set professionals apart in an AI-powered world. Again, you can get all the exercises from this chapter by downloading our free workbook at ownyourbrandbook.com.

1. Emotional Intelligence

We talked about EQ as the ability to read yourself before you try to read the room. Reflect on this and ask:

- What are three things you can express gratitude for, right now?

- Think of a moment when you felt overwhelmed, frustrated, or emotionally off. What patterns do you tend to fall into when you feel this way?

2. Judgment & Critical Thinking

Think of a time you had to make a decision without a clear right answer. What was the hardest part about making that call, and what did you learn from it?

- When outcomes don't go as planned, how did you respond or adjust to them?
- What's a field or discipline you could learn from that might sharpen your thinking under pressure?

3. Storytelling

Think of some of your favorite stories, from any medium.

- What stories stick with you—and why, do you think?
- What moved you?
- What in the story made you feel something?

4. Collaboration & Inclusion

Think of a time when a project got stuck, misunderstood, or slowed down because people weren't on the same page. Reflect and ask:

- Whose perspective were you and the team missing?
- How might someone with a different background have seen the project?

- What assumptions were you or others making that might have limited progress?

5. Adaptability

Think of a recent change or disruption that forced you to adjust at work. Reflect on it and try to:

- Adopt a learning mindset by asking, "What could I learn here?"
- Test small changes, like a new tool, workflow, or approach
- Learn from new people: cross-pollinate ideas from other teams or industries

6. Resilience

Think of a challenge or setback that knocked you off course. Reflect on it and ask:

- What's good about this?
- What can I learn from it?
- What does this make possible?
- What's in my control, and what's not?

7. Taste & Discernment

- **Try to curate what you consume.** Your inputs shape your instincts. Follow creators, designers, filmmakers, thinkers, and chefs whose work you admire. Be intentional about who fills your feeds online and what fills your mind offline.

- **Pay attention to what resonates with you.** When something moves you, stop and ask why: was it the framing of the shot in the film? The meaningful way a character gave a certain speech? The brightness of the focal point in a photo? The immediacy of the imagery in a sentence? Just try to notice and think about what's good and what's not.

- **Edit your own life.** The way you dress; decorate your home; plan your day; write an email; or present a deck. These are all reflections of taste. Ask yourself:

  - What feels cluttered?
  - What feels clear?
  - What feels like *me*?

- **Study great work.** Rewatch your favorite film with the director's commentary. Read the same paragraph several times and try to notice the rhythm of the language. Your taste can improve when you study the decisions that led to the creation of a great work.

- **Practice subtraction.** Taste often shows up in what's not there. A great design doesn't have too much, and a good speech doesn't say everything. Try to train yourself to say more with less.

- **Ask people with good taste to critique your work.** Whether it's writing, design, presentations, or even your wardrobe, get feedback from those whose eye you respect. You'll see more clearly through theirs.

In the next chapter, we'll explore how to leverage LinkedIn beyond a digital resume: as a platform for showcasing the deeply human qualities that set you apart. The fact is that the best personal brand in the world means nothing if it's invisible.

CHAPTER SIX:

HOW TO LEVERAGE LINKEDIN TO BUILD YOUR BRAND

LinkedIn launched in 2003 as a digital resume and basic networking tool. For years, that's mostly how people used it—to connect with former colleagues, list job titles, and maybe find a new role. But in the last few years, with new owner Microsoft's shepherding, the platform has evolved; today it's the most powerful professional platform in the world, with over a billion users and rising.

While many people still treat it as a place to update their job history or scroll through news, high performers use LinkedIn differently: they use it to position their brand, build relationships, and create visibility that leads to genuine opportunities. And, in our opinion, there is no better place to be connecting with others and building your personal and professional brand.

This chapter is about doing just that. We'll walk you through how to shape your profile, engage with your network, and share your voice in a way that elevates your brand and creates traction—without feeling fake, sales-y, or overwhelming. (We think there's a lot of value in that.)

LINKEDIN BASICS

Your LinkedIn profile is a little like a storefront. If you walk by a restaurant and the lights are off, the sign is faded, and the parking lot is empty, you'll probably keep walking, right? It doesn't matter how good the food might be inside—if the outside doesn't signal that it's worth checking out, most people will never walk through the door.

Your profile is the same way: it's your first impression, and whether you realize it or not, it shapes how people perceive you. That's why it's so important to be serious about filling out your profile completely.

Start with a solid profile photo. The simplest and most effective option is a professional headshot where you're looking into the camera and smiling. This doesn't have to be a glamor shot, but it should be clear, well-lit, and not a selfie. You can absolutely express your personality here, but aim for something that strikes a balance between polished and approachable. Not sure what that looks like? Browse around LinkedIn to see what kinds of photos give off the right mix of professional and friendly. And feel free to find our profiles there and follow or connect with us as well!

Next, look at your background photo: the banner image at the top of your profile. You can keep it simple with one of LinkedIn's default images, but it's better if you personalize it. This could be a photo of you in action (speaking, working, or even leading), a visual that aligns with your company or brand, or a custom-designed graphic that quickly communicates what you do. Think of this as the sign on your window—it tells people what's inside.

Once you've got the visual elements sorted, it's time to focus on the words that will do most of the heavy lifting.

THE HEADLINE

This is the short line of text that appears right under your name, and it's one of the most valuable pieces of real estate on your entire profile. It's often the only thing people read when they visit a profile.

If you don't customize it, LinkedIn will just pull in your job title and company by default (e.g., "Data Analyst at Zurich Insurance"), which doesn't say much. But if you think about it a little, you can turn this into a mini billboard that quickly shows who you are and the value you can bring to a company or project.

Recently, I (Andy) looked up a connection who works in learning and development. His headline could've just been his title and company, but instead, he wrote:

"Director of Learning and Organizational Development who helps organizations increase productivity by improving team effectiveness and maximizing the talents of individual employees."

This clearly goes far beyond a title: it tells us what he *actually* does, and who benefits. If a recruiter or potential collaborator came across his profile, they'd immediately see how he could help an organization.

Another connection of mine who also works in the talent development space put "Talent Whisperer" in her headline, and it was the first thing I asked about when we got on a call recently. I wanted to know where that came from and why it was there. It was an excellent conversation starter.

If you wear multiple hats, feel free to include more than one role or focus area using vertical bars, dividers, or commas.

At the time of this writing, Andy's headline reads:

Keynote Speaker & Facilitator | Career, Personal Brand & Leadership Expert | Author Own Your Career Own Your Life | 🎥 Talent Development Podcast & Community host | Cancer Survivor, Father, Cyclist, Ally 🎥

Here's what the whole thing looks like together:

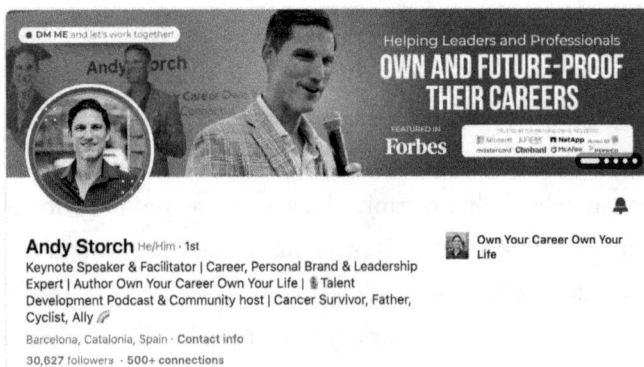

Mike's reads:

WSJ Bestselling Author, "You Are the Brand" as Featured in Entrepreneur, Inc. ■ Personal Branding Expert for Executives, Experts, and Entrepreneurs

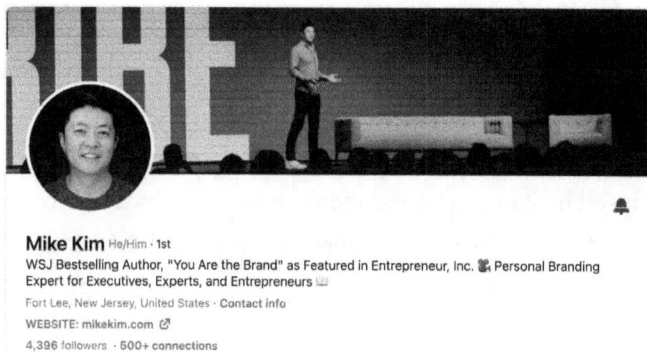

Mike Kim He/Him · 1st
WSJ Bestselling Author, "You Are the Brand" as Featured in Entrepreneur, Inc. 📸 Personal Branding Expert for Executives, Experts, and Entrepreneurs 📖
Fort Lee, New Jersey, United States · Contact info
WEBSITE: mikekim.com ⌐⊃
4,396 followers · 500+ connections

A great thing about LinkedIn is that nothing is set in stone. Your headline can (and should) evolve as you do. We change ours all the time. So just review it every few months, take some inspiration from others, and don't be afraid to experiment until it feels like you.

Now that your headline is working for you, let's make sure your work history tells the right story.

YOUR EXPERIENCE

You don't have to spend hours on this, but here are a few things to keep in mind:

1. FOCUS ON WHAT SUPPORTS YOUR PERSONAL BRAND.

You don't need to include every job you've ever held.

If you worked as a lifeguard or server in college and it has no relevance to what you do now, leave it off. Any professional roles, especially those that show progression or transferable skills, should be included.

2. TELL US WHAT YOU ACTUALLY ACCOMPLISHED.

Don't just copy and paste your job description. Instead of saying "Responsible for managing backend systems," try something more specific and results-oriented like:

"Revamped backend systems to increase processing speed by 25 percent and reduce team costs by 20 percent."

One or two clear bullet points like that can make quite a difference.

3. DON'T BE AFRAID TO INCLUDE TIME SPENT OUT OF THE TRADITIONAL WORKFORCE.

If you stepped away to be a full-time parent or caretaker, that's part of your professional story, and we recommend you own it. You can include this with a fun title like "Chief Household Officer" or "Full-Time Caregiver" and add a short, proud description. You shouldn't be embarrassed about it; not at all.

One of our favorites was "Raised and wrangled small colleagues while managing logistics, education, and emotional development—true executive leadership in action."

Some people just put "professional break."

This is part of your journey, though, and you may as well take pride and have fun with it, rather than hide it, which will just cause potential hiring managers to wonder, perhaps not in the best way—or ask you about it anyway.

4. ADD YOUR CERTIFICATIONS, DEGREES, AND RELEVANT TRAINING.

LinkedIn has sections for education and credentials, and while you don't have to list everything, include anything relevant to your career or the message you want to send. If you've completed recent trainings or earned certifications, this is the place to include them.

Remember that apart from being a sort of resume, your Experience section is a curated story of where you've been, what you've done, and how it shapes the work you're doing now. Keep it focused, honest, and easy to scan.

FIVE WAYS TO MAKE YOUR EXPERIENCE SECTION STAND OUT

1. USE FIRST PERSON TO SOUND MORE HUMAN

Instead of writing like a resume, use a conversational, first-person tone. Example: "In this role, I led a team of five analysts to redesign our reporting workflows, which cut delivery time by 40 percent." This reads more like a story than a bullet list and makes you more approachable.

2. ADD MEDIA TO HIGHLIGHT YOUR WORK

LinkedIn allows you to upload documents, images, videos, links, and presentations in each job entry. If you've done a keynote, written an article, launched a product, or created a portfolio, add a link or file. This helps bring your experience to life and adds visual proof of your work.

3. USE KEYWORDS FOR DISCOVERABILITY

Recruiters and hiring managers search by keywords, so think about that. Look at job descriptions in your field and use relevant language: tools, certifications, methodologies, or industries. If you've worked with Salesforce, Hubspot, or Agile teams, mention it. Speak the language of your industry.

4. SHOW CAREER PROGRESSION, EVEN WITHIN THE SAME COMPANY

If you've had multiple roles at one company, break them out as separate entries under the same organization. For example:

- Marketing Associate (2019–2021)
- Senior Marketing Manager (2021–Present)

This shows growth while also giving you space to highlight new accomplishments in each role.

5. MATCH YOUR PROFILE TO YOUR CURRENT GOALS

Your experience section should support where you're going instead of just recounting where you've been. If you're pivoting to a new industry or function, try to reframe your past experiences to highlight transferable skills; instead of just listing tasks, show how your previous work prepared you for the value you bring now.

For example, if you're transitioning from teaching into corporate learning and development, instead of saying:

"Taught high school math and managed classroom activities,"

You might say:

"Designed and facilitated engaging learning experiences for diverse audiences, developed curriculum aligned with performance goals, and coached individuals to achieve measurable growth—skills now applied to corporate training and employee development."

This kind of reframing helps connect your past roles to your future goals, making it easier for others to see the value you bring.

"ABOUT" SECTION

This part can feel tricky because it requires writing about yourself in a way that's both compelling and clear. Before diving in, we recommend browsing profiles of others in your industry to get a feel for how people are using this space and to take note of what stands out.

Think of the "About" section as your elevator pitch. It's a short summary that explains who you are, what you do, the value you bring, and maybe even what else you're interested in. There's no perfect formula, but a good "About" section gives a quick snapshot of your professional identity.

You'll see some people write in the third person, like a formal bio. That's perfectly fine—but don't be afraid to write in the first person either ("I help…" or "My work focuses on…") especially if you want your tone to feel more personal and approachable.

You can write a short narrative, list bullet points, highlight career successes, or even share a bit of your backstory. There are no hard rules, but just aim to be clear, relevant, and a little human. Most people will be skimming, so make sure they can quickly grasp who you are and why your work matters. Here are four styles that may work for you:

1. NARRATIVE STYLE (CONVERSATIONAL, FIRST-PERSON)

I'm a talent development and communications professional with a passion for helping teams grow and thrive. Over the last decade, I've led internal culture initiatives, built leadership development programs, and supported employees through key career transitions—all within fast-paced corporate environments.

I believe great workplaces are built from the inside out, and that people do their best work when they feel supported and understood.

When I'm not working, you'll probably find me on a hiking trail, deep in a book, or fine-tuning my morning coffee routine.

2. IMPACT STYLE (STRONG OUTCOMES AND VALUE)

I lead strategic marketing initiatives that drive measurable results across the business.

Currently managing digital campaigns at [Company

Name], where we've:

- Boosted qualified leads by 42 percent year over year
- Launched three major campaigns across North America
- Reduced customer acquisition costs by 35 percent

My focus areas include cross-channel marketing, paid media, and aligning product messaging with customer insights.

I thrive at the intersection of strategy and execution, and I'm known for making complex projects feel simple and seamless.

3. HYBRID STYLE (PROFESSIONAL BUT HUMAN)

This strikes a balance between resume-worthy content and personality:

Strategic communicator and collaborative team player with a passion for simplifying the complex.

Over the past ten years, I've worked across internal communications, corporate marketing, and employee engagement—supporting company-wide initiatives that connect people to purpose and drive clarity across teams. Whether leading internal messaging for a product launch or crafting materials for leadership, I focus on making communication clear, human, and actionable.

I believe great strategy starts with empathy, and effective leadership starts with listening.

Always open to connecting with others who care

about building thoughtful, high-impact work cultures.

4. QUICK BULLET STYLE (MINIMALIST)

Perfect for scanners and people who prefer to keep things tight:

WHAT I DO:

- Drive cross-functional projects from strategy to execution
- Improve internal processes to boost team efficiency
- Translate complex goals into actionable plans

WHO I SUPPORT:

- Mid-size to enterprise teams
- Operations, HR, and strategy departments

OPEN TO:

- Internal mentoring
- Cross-functional collaboration
- Leadership development opportunities

These optional elements can add extra credibility, but they're not essential. What matters most is having the fundamentals in place.

Please note that LinkedIn formatting does not work with standard bulletpoints: it is necessary to use the Unicode/ASCII symbols for them to work on your profile, as we do here.

FEATURED SECTION AND RECOMMENDATIONS

The last (and more optional) parts of your profile to consider are the Featured section and Recommendations.

The Featured section lets you highlight content that showcases who you are and what you care about. This could be a blog post, video, portfolio, podcast, nonprofit, personal website, or anything else you want people to explore. You might think of it as a small spotlight where you direct attention to the work or ideas that matter most to you.

Recommendations are testimonials from people you've worked with, like clients, colleagues, mentors, managers, or direct reports. While not required, having a few solid recommendations gives you more credibility. You can always write a few for others and then kindly ask if they'd be willing to return the favor.

Here are three short, effective, and professional ways to request a recommendation:

- Hi [Name], I really enjoyed working together on [project/team]. Would you be open to writing a brief LinkedIn recommendation about our work? I'd be happy to return the favor.

- Hi [Name], I'm updating my LinkedIn profile and would truly appreciate a short recommendation from you, especially around our time working on [specific responsibility/project]. Let me know if you're open to it.

- Hi [Name], You've had a big impact on my growth at [company name], and I'd be honored if you'd write a quick recommendation highlighting our work together. Thanks for considering it.

If someone agrees to write a recommendation for you but isn't sure where to start, make it easy for them. You can offer one of the following templates as a helpful starting point. Each one can be tailored based on your relationship and the tone you want to strike. You can also use these yourself when writing recommendations for others—just plug in the details, personalize a few lines, and you're good to go.

THREE RECOMMENDATION TEMPLATES

1. COLLABORATIVE COLLEAGUE TEMPLATE

Great for teammates or peers you worked closely with:

I had the pleasure of working with [Your Name] on [specific project/team] at [Company Name], and they consistently impressed me with their [mention strengths—e.g., attention to detail, communication, creative thinking].

What stood out most was [his/her/their] ability to [specific result or strength]. [Your Name] is a true team player who elevates everyone around them, and I would gladly work with [him/her/them] again in a heartbeat.

2. MANAGER OR SUPERVISOR TEMPLATE

For bosses who oversaw your work or performance:

[Your Name] reported to me during our time at [Company Name], and it was clear from day one that [he/she/they] brought not just skill, but genuine ownership and initiative to the role.

One example that stands out is when [Your Name] [describe a standout moment, result, or project]. That kind of impact, combined with [his/her/their] professionalism and work ethic, made [him/her/them] a key asset to our team. Any organization would be lucky to have [him/her/them].

3. DIRECT REPORT OR MENTEE TEMPLATE

If someone you led is writing about you, this helps structure their thoughts:

I had the opportunity to work under [Your Name]'s leadership at [Company Name], and it was one of the most positive professional experiences of my career.

[He/She/They] led with clarity, empathy, and high standards, always ensuring that we had the support and direction we needed to succeed. I especially appreciated how [he/she/they] [specific leadership trait or example]. [Your Name] helped me grow, and I'm better for it.

CONNECTIONS: SLIDE INTO THEIR DMS (BUT PROFESSIONALLY)

One of the most fundamental parts of LinkedIn is, of course, connecting. Some might say that was the whole point when it started: to connect with people you've worked with so you could keep in touch professionally. But obviously it's more than that today.

You can connect with people you've worked with, gone to school with, met at events, or simply admire and want to learn from.

If you haven't been active on LinkedIn or built up your network over the years, don't stress. Like the old proverb says, "The best time to plant a tree was 20 years ago. The second best time is today."

Start by sending connection requests to people you've worked with, studied with, or interacted with in any meaningful way. This includes colleagues, classmates, mentors, clients, or folks you've met at conferences or workshops.

There's very little downside to connecting. Unlike Facebook or other social platforms, LinkedIn tends to be more professional and reserved, so you're fairly unlikely to see the kind of content that causes conflict. If for some reason you change your mind, you can always remove a connection later.

As of this writing, the maximum number of connections you can have is 30,000. That's quite a generous ceiling, and most of us won't come anywhere near it, so be proactive. You never know when a connection might lead to a conversation, opportunity, or a future collaboration.

THE ART OF THE CONNECTION REQUEST

When you send a connection request, take the extra 15 seconds to add a personal note. It doesn't need to be long or fancy—just a quick line to remind the person how you know each other, or why you'd like to connect. If there's any chance the person may not remember who you are, add a note with some context such as:

- "Hey Taylor, I loved your insights during last week's team meeting. Would love to stay connected here."

- "Hi Jordan, we met at the Austin conference in March—it was great chatting with you about leadership development."

- "Hi Sam, I've been following your work on talent strategy. I would love to connect and learn more."

- "April, it's been a long time since we worked together, and thought we could benefit from connecting here."

- "Nancy, since we already work together IRL, I thought we could connect here as well."

- "Hey Jenny, I just realized we are not connected here—let's change that!"

Adding a personal note helps your request stand out, shows that you mean what you're doing, and starts the conversation on the right foot. It's a small gesture, but can go a long way in building real connection. It also helps you remember how you got connected in the first place.

Once you've connected with people you already know, the next step is to start building relationships with people you don't know yet but would benefit from knowing. This could include people in your industry, professionals doing the kind of work you'd like to do, or potential mentors who inspire you.

Most people on LinkedIn are open to connecting if it's clear you have genuine intentions.

A good place to start is the search bar. Type in a job title, company, or industry—then click "People" and filter by location or shared connections. For example, you might search for "senior data analyst" in your city and find dozens of professionals doing work that interests you.

You can then send a personalized request like:

- "Hi Sarah, I saw you're a senior data analyst at XYZ Company. I'm working in data too, and would love to connect and learn from others in the space."

You can also look up alumni from your university or past employers. People are far more likely to connect with you if they sense shared experiences or values.

Note: The free version of LinkedIn offers enough search tools to get started, but if you ever want to filter by company size, seniority, or additional criteria, you can upgrade to LinkedIn Premium. For now, just use what's available to you and focus on thoughtful outreach.

Once someone accepts your request, don't let the trail go cold. Send a quick message to say thanks and consider starting a conversation. If it's an old colleague, suggest a "virtual coffee" catch-up call. If it's someone new, you might offer a brief chat to learn more about their career path or share your own.

We've both made some of our best professional connections this way, and many have turned into real friendships.

THREE WAYS TO ENGAGE STRATEGICALLY

Once your profile is updated and your network is growing, the next step is to start showing up consistently, intentionally, and authentically. This is where many people get it wrong. They assume they need to start writing thought leadership posts or sharing original articles immediately.

While that can be helpful later, it's not the only (or even the best) place to begin. A more approachable and effective first step is to engage with other people's content. Here's how to do that:

1. FOLLOW VOICES IN YOUR INDUSTRY.

Search for people in your field who regularly post content. This might include colleagues, industry leaders, or people who do the kind of work you want to do. Click "Follow" on their profiles to make sure you see their content in your feed.

2. START LIKING POSTS THAT RESONATE.

Engaging with posts you genuinely enjoy signals to LinkedIn's algorithm what kind of content is relevant to you. Over time, this helps tailor your feed so you see more posts that align with your interests.

Every time you hit "like," that engagement shows up in your activity feed and may also surface in the feeds of your connections. Your likes are little breadcrumbs that lead people back to your profile. Instead of mindlessly liking everything you scroll past, focus on posts that reflect your values, your voice, or your area of expertise. Each interaction is a small brand-building moment.

3. LEAVE THOUGHTFUL COMMENTS.

Writing a genuine, insightful comment can often get you more visibility than posting something of your own. It also signals to the original poster (and their audience) that you're engaged, informed, and worth paying attention to.

Aim for comments that add perspective, ask a good question, or share a relevant experience. A few examples:

- "This is such a great point about team dynamics. We've been running into something similar. Curious how you handled XYZ?"

- "I hadn't thought about it that way. Thanks for sharing this insight, it's changing how I think about [topic]."

- "I've been experimenting with something similar. Here's what worked for us..."

You don't need to be on LinkedIn for hours a day. Even 10–15 minutes a few times a week can help. Just try to make engagement a habit, not a one-time effort.

You might have more time for this than you think. Commutes, waiting rooms, lunch breaks, and even the time spent scrolling through social media can be repurposed for LinkedIn. Instead of defaulting to passive content or background noise, small windows of time can be opportunities for commenting on a post, replying to a message, or just following a new voice in your field.

Richard Larson at MIT conducted a study and found the average person will spend two full years worth of time waiting in line. (Depressing, we know.) But that time doesn't have to disappear: if we think about it when we're in the moment, we can use it to build real momentum—all without ever needing to hit "publish" on a post.

People will begin to recognize your name. They'll associate you with smart, respectful input. And when the time comes for you to share your own content, you'll already have an audience that's paying attention.

If you can be consistent, LinkedIn creates a flywheel effect—profile views lead to connections, connections lead to conversations, and conversations lead to opportunities.

That's the power of being strategic about your LinkedIn presence—it's about putting effort into your time there and what value you bring to the professional conversations happening every day.

Phew! We covered a lot in this chapter. As always, you can get all the templates and exercises from this chapter by downloading the free workbook at ownyourbrandbook.com. There's also a checklist there to keep you on track in making all your LinkedIn updates.

In the next chapter, we'll move beyond building your profile and connections to jump into the heart of your visibility: sharing your ideas, experiences, and insights in ways that build trust and keep you at the top of others' minds.

CHAPTER SEVEN:
CONTENT THAT SHOWCASES YOUR EXPERTISE AND AMPLIFIES YOUR INFLUENCE

Actor Steve Carell is best known for playing the hilariously awkward Michael Scott on The Office: it was one of the iconic comedy roles of its time. But after several seasons, Carell wanted to shift gears, take on more serious roles, and reinvent how people saw him.

As you might imagine, that kind of pivot isn't easy. Audiences typecast actors, and comedians aren't always taken seriously; transitioning from television to film can be a risky leap. Carell stopped taking comedy roles and stepped back from the talk show circuit where people would inevitably ask about The Office, and then, seemingly out of nowhere, he reemerged in *Foxcatcher*—a dark, dramatic film that earned him an Academy Award nomination.

Carell took a chance at changing his perception by

working differently. Sure, he stepped away from public view for a while, but reemerged to shape the narrative by creating something new. That's the power of content.

Matthew McConaughey famously made a similarly unlikely change from being the king of romantic comedies in the early 2000s to doing more serious films like *Dallas Buyers Club* and *Interstellar*. He wrote all about his journey and his steadfast intention to change despite industry pressure against it in his bestselling book *Greenlights*.

The content you put out can be one the clearest signals of who you are and who you're becoming. The more that people see your name and face in their feed, the more likely they are to remember you and associate you with your area of interest or expertise. The moment you share something thoughtful, someone in your network might comment, DM you, or introduce you to someone else. At the very least, it will get filed away in their brains and reinforced later when they see your content again.

We've both had moments where someone at a live event says, "I've seen your posts online." That kind of recognition builds instant familiarity and helps deepen relationships much faster. We know people who got job interviews just from one post on LinkedIn or other content they've created because it resonated with a hiring manager who then reached out.

One of the most underrated benefits of creating content is that it helps you get clear about who you are yourself. The more you reflect on what you're learning and how you're growing, the more clarity you gain about what you stand for, what gets you excited, and what kind of work you want to do more of. That kind of focus is worth more than gold when you're exploring new roles or trying to grow your career.

Before you start worrying about what to post or whether it will land perfectly, it helps to know that almost all valuable content falls into just a few basic categories.

THE THREE WAYS TO PROVIDE VALUE THROUGH CONTENT

Almost all valuable content falls into one of three categories: entertainment, education, or inspiration.

- **Entertainment:** Content that's funny, relatable, or enjoyable simply makes someone's day better. It builds connection by creating positive emotions.

- **Education:** Content that teaches something useful, like a new idea, tip, or perspective, positions you as a helpful, informed resource.

- **Inspiration:** Content that shares lessons you've learned, personal growth, or encouragement gives others motivation or courage to take action in their own lives.

You don't have to master all three: many people naturally lean toward one or two. For example, most of the content Andy shares falls into the "inspiration" bucket.

Mike's posts fall mostly into education. When you focus on creating value in at least one of these three ways, you give people a reason to keep engaging with you—and you gradually build trust, credibility, and visibility without feeling like you're "selling" yourself.

Before diving into specific tactics, let's look at the foundation of all great content: storytelling.

THE EVERYDAY WAY TO TELL STORIES

People have been communicating and conveying information via stories for thousands of years, and even today, nearly every social media app has followed the short-form "stories" features pioneered by Snapchat and then adopted Instagram—which means that the population at large is becoming more and more aware of the principles behind storytelling.

It's easy to think that great storytelling is a rare talent reserved for naturally gifted writers or orators—but storytelling is more natural than you might realize, and can be learned by anyone. You don't need to become the next Shakespeare or Oscar-winning screenwriter; instead, just try to focus on mastering a few important principles that can elevate your communication skills. Let's look at Aristotle to learn an important framework on dramatic structure and storytelling:

Any standard, good story involves a character who experiences an "inciting incident" that sets the rest of the tale into motion. If you've ever listened to someone ramble through a dinner story and thought, "Ugh, just get to the point," it's usually because they're taking too long to get to that spark. We often get in our own way when writing stories because we get into "writing mode," and it's no surprise. For most of our lives, we were taught in school to write essays, which are not stories.

When we share stories in real life, we naturally start at the inciting incident—whether good, bad, or neutral. Let's say a loved one asks you how work was. You might say something like:

- "You'll never guess what Andy and Mike did in today's meeting! Ugh!"

- "When I was getting out of the car this morning, I dropped my phone and it broke…"

- "While I was leaving work, my boss pulled me into the office and asked me point-blank how much I want to be paid to become Chief Marketing Officer of the company!"

The key here is to start at the spark and lead with the inciting incident. The inciting incident is one of the most important elements of storytelling: it's the spark that gets the story moving. A good story starts where the change begins—where something unexpected happened or something clicked. That moment is what pulls people in and gets them curious.

The good news is your stories don't have to be epic: all you need is a simple incident that sets things into motion. Once you understand how stories work, the next step is deciding which perspective you want to share them from.

SAGE, SHERPA, STRUGGLER: THREE PERSPECTIVES TO SHARE YOUR EXPERTISE

Bestselling author and former CEO of Thomas Nelson books, Michael Hyatt, says there are three different perspectives one can share their expertise from: the Sage, the Sherpa, and the Struggler. Each offers a unique and valuable way to share your knowledge and experiences, and they all work nicely with the storytelling framework we just covered.

THE SAGE: THE EXPERT PERSPECTIVE

The Sage is an expert who has reached the pinnacle of knowledge in a particular field. This person stands at the top of a mountain, sharing wisdom and insights from a place of authority. They don't have to be famous or have millions of followers, but they do need to have the credentials and body of work to support their position.

For example, if you have extensive experience in project management and have received a senior or C-level position you've held for a long time, you could share advanced strategies and methodologies that help others improve their own project execution.

THE SHERPA: THE GUIDE PERSPECTIVE

The Sherpa is someone who has walked a path before and knows the terrain well. This guide shares practical advice and tips from personal experience. Imagine a seasoned professional who has navigated the challenges of career progression and is now offering guidance to those just starting out, all while continuing to grow.

As a Sherpa, your role is to demystify processes, provide actionable steps, and support others as they embark on similar journeys. You might share tips on effective networking, lessons learned from overcoming career setbacks, or insights on balancing work and personal life.

Keep in mind that a "seasoned" professional does not necessarily mean you have to be a corporate executive with 25+ years of experience. Everything is relative.

Even a 25-year old with 2-3 years of work experience is a seasoned veteran with lots of expertise compared with someone just coming out of college trying to learn the ins and outs of the corporate world.

THE STRUGGLER: THE PEER PERSPECTIVE

The Struggler is right there in the trenches, facing the same challenges as their peers, community, or audience. This perspective is about sharing your journey, including the ups and downs, and providing a relatable voice.

By acknowledging your struggles, you offer a sense of solidarity and encouragement to others going through similar experiences. If you're working on improving your public speaking skills, you could share updates about your progress, the obstacles you've faced, and the small victories you've maybe had along the way. This makes your content approachable and authentic, which promotes a connection with your audience. And it will be highly relatable to many people, as public speaking is often cited as the number-one fear for most people.

Now that you understand the fundamentals of storytelling and perspective, let's address the elephant in the room: AI tools that can help with content creation.

BE AUTHENTIC

The world "authentic" is almost overused these days—but as we've stated before, humans like to connect with other humans, and as AI and technology does more and more, humans want to connect with *and learn* from other humans. So really, please don't be afraid to be your true self: even on LinkedIn.

For example, Lea Turner has openly shared her journey on LinkedIn as a tattooed single mother with ADHD. She never tried to cater to the expected professional "norms" of LinkedIn. Instead, she shared openly about her wins, challenges, and life, and as a result, she's attracted a following of over 175,000 on LinkedIn and a highly engaged community of entrepreneurs (www.theholt.com) who look to her for guidance, insights, and connection.

"I've always shown up exactly as I am—tattoos, ADHD, single parent, neurodivergent, messy past—and I've never tried to water that down for LinkedIn. The more myself I was, the more people connected with me."

This approach has opened doors for so many others to show up more authentically. As Lea says "When one person loosens the tie, the next person does... and suddenly we're all sitting around really relaxed, having a genuine conversation."

When we asked Lea for advice about what types of content to share on LinkedIn, she said to just think about the person you were five, ten, or even 15 years ago and start giving that person advice. "If I had seen myself 15 years ago, I'd be a lot further ahead than I am now."

SHOULD YOU USE AI?

The short answer is yes, of course, but we want to caution you to do so carefully.

AI can help you brainstorm ideas, structure your thoughts, and draft initial outlines of whatever you're working on. But AI can't replicate your perspective, experiences, or the unique way you see the world.

Your personal brand is built on your authenticity: people connect to your voice, stories, and point of view. Those are things only *you* can provide. People don't want to feel like they're reading through engagement-minded nonsense; they want to connect with someone.

So, we recommend that you use AI as a thinking partner, instead of a replacement for your own brain. It can seriously help you get unstuck or organize your ideas, but make sure what you publish sounds like you, and not like everyone else using the same prompts.

GETTING STARTED: THREE SIMPLE WAYS

With that in mind, let's start with three simple, low-pressure ways to begin creating content that really feels like it's yours.

1. SHARE WHAT YOU'RE READING, LEARNING, OR LISTENING TO

If you're already reading industry articles, newsletters, or books, you're halfway to building content. One of the easiest ways to stay visible on LinkedIn is by simply sharing what you're consuming and adding a quick thought of your own. We recommend it; it takes very little effort. Aren't we always consuming some kind of media that might be interesting for others?

For example, if you read an article, you could post something like:

"Just finished this article on how AI is reshaping the hiring process. The author's point about bias in algorithms really stood out, especially for those of us in HR. Worth a read if you are navigating these shifts too."

This signals that you're staying current and thinking critically, and that you may be someone others could learn from. It also reinforces that you're engaged in your industry and committed to learning.

Something else you can do is post short book reviews. We think this is something not done enough, but it can be an easy, meaningful way to stand out. If you read regularly (or even just occasionally), posting a few thoughts when you finish a book can build your brand as someone who is thoughtful, engaged, and always learning. It doesn't have to be anything complicated, just something as simple as:

"I just finished reading *Own Your Brand, Own Your Career* and really enjoyed it because it gave me a lot of practical ideas about how to be more intentional with my career growth. Highly recommend if you are thinking about your next career move."

When you post about the books you're reading, it provides valuable recommendations for others—something most people appreciate—as well as subtly shows that you're a learner and someone who invests in yourself.

2. SHARE A QUOTE OR INSIGHT

A quote or thoughtful insight can offer quick value to your network. No need to be profound or poetic—just try to keep it relevant. Sharing a brief insight from your workweek signals that you're thoughtful, reflective, and able to connect ideas to your real-world experience. You can pull from a meeting, a conversation, or something you learned. An example:

"Technology is best when it brings people together."—Matt Mullenweg

We're deep in system upgrades at work this month, and this quote reminded me why we're doing it. Tools are only as good as the collaboration they support.

3. TELL A TINY STORY

Think of something that happened at work recently—a success or a lesson, perhaps a challenge—and distill it down. An example:

"I used to dread giving updates during team meetings. Then one day, I flipped the script and started framing my updates as stories: what problem we were solving, what changed, and what happened. Suddenly, people were listening. Sometimes small shifts make a big impact."

You don't need to do all of these at once. Just pick one format and try it once this week. The goal in this case is merely to build momentum. Just getting started is the hardest part, and then you can learn and grow from there.

THE THREE PS FRAMEWORK

While starting is often the hardest part, some people like having a framework to follow. One we like comes from Kait LeDonne, a personal branding expert who coaches thought leaders to build a stronger brand on LinkedIn. When Andy interviewed her to get her tips on building a strong personal brand, Kait shared her "Three P's" framework that she uses with her clients:

- **Professional (60%):** Show your expertise and the value you deliver. This could be based on your job, your industry, your experience, or things you are learning about.

- **Passion (20%):** Causes or communities you care deeply about. This could be a non-profit, personal development, or things you are learning, or helping others, and so on.

- **Personal/Personable (20%):** Relatable stories, values, and personality. A lot of people think LinkedIn content has to be "professional", but humans like connecting with other humans, and the best content is often personal and relatable.

Liam Darmody, a LinkedIn expert and personal brand strategist, has a similar framework. He says he advises people to share content in three buckets:

1. **Skills** – Share what you're good at, professional insights, and industry knowledge.

2. **Fascination** – Topics that excite you and show your passions.

3. **Window into Your World** – Light, personal stories that help people relate to you.

With that in mind, here is a simple content plan that can help you get started:

A SIMPLE CONTENT PLAN ANYONE CAN FOLLOW

Once you've dipped your toe into content sharing, the next step is being consistent. Here's a simple weekly structure anyone can follow for LinkedIn, especially if you're just starting out:

MONDAY: SHARE AN ARTICLE OR SOMETHING VALUABLE YOU READ OR WATCHED

Start the week with something valuable to your network. Find an article, podcast, or short video relevant to your field and repost it to your own feed with a short comment:

"Just read this piece on remote team engagement. Great reminder that we build company culture every day, and not only during all-hands meetings. I'm curious how others are keeping teams connected across time zones?"

TUESDAY: POST A QUOTE OR BRIEF INSIGHT

This can be as simple as a favorite quote that relates to work, leadership, or personal development—or a line from something you're reading.

"Leadership is not about being in charge. It's about taking care of those in your charge."—Simon Sinek

This one hit me today, especially as I step into managing a new team.

WEDNESDAY OR THURSDAY: TELL A TINY STORY

This is your "midweek moment." Share a tiny work-related reflection. It might be something you learned, observed, or experienced.

We had a hiccup in a client presentation today: mid-slide, our video froze. But instead of panic, our team paused, regrouped, and moved on it. It reminded me that resilience isn't about being perfect—it's more like being adaptable and able to roll with the punches. Big shout-out to Duane, Chelsea, and Jason!

One important lesson we've learned over the years is that if you are struggling with something or had an "ah ha" moment lately, chances are there are thousands (if not millions!) of others who can relate and learn from the same thing. We are more similar than we realize.

FRIDAY: SUPPORT SOMEONE ELSE

Instead of posting your own content, use Fridays to lift others up. Maybe you can congratulate a teammate on a milestone, or share thoughtful comments on other posts. This builds goodwill, strengthens your network, and shows you're collaborative.

If you keep doing this, you'll start to stand out as someone who adds value, and people will start associating your name with ideas, insights, and leadership.

If you've already been posting for a while, scroll through your last 30 days of content. Do you think your posts reflect who you are and the direction you want to go? If not, make some adjustments. Your content is like a radio station or a carefully-curated playlist. If people tune in expecting jazz and suddenly get heavy metal, they'll probably change the channel. The same goes for your posts. When one day you're sharing leadership insights and the next you're venting about traffic, your audience won't know what to expect and may stop paying attention.

Before posting, try to ask yourself: Is this useful? Is this thoughtful? Does this reflect how I want to be perceived? These simple questions help keep your brand consistent.

Once you've established a consistent rhythm with basic content, you might be ready to explore more ambitious projects that can significantly amplify your personal brand.

START A PODCAST OR YOUTUBE CHANNEL

Launching a podcast or YouTube channel might feel like a big step, but it is one of the fastest ways to build your personal brand and expand your network. You don't need to be an expert; you just, again, need to be consistent—one of the golden rules of social media use—and to stay open to both new ideas and new perspectives on old ones.

Some of the most recognizable names in media are not experts in the fields they cover. For example: Joe Rogan almost never knows more than his guests, but he built credibility by staying consistent, asking good questions, and curating conversations that felt meaningful. Though he unfortunately sometimes courts falsehoods, conspiracies, and half-truths on his show, he's a great example of an very well-known interview host whose interviewees essentially always know more about their subject than he does (except regarding Mixed Martial Arts, or MMA, as he worked extensively in professional fighting and adjacent areas). You might be able to build a name for yourself without relevant specialization, as well.

It's good to start with what interests you: if you're in HR, maybe you could interview leaders about people development trends. If you're in tech, maybe you could talk to product managers about building solid digital experiences. You don't need a massive budget or fancy gear: just a basic microphone, Zoom, and a format people can easily grasp. Your perspective, and keeping at it, are the most important things.

One of the advantages of starting a show is that you build credibility by association. If you interview respected voices in your industry, some of their authority will naturally reflect onto you. Over time, you'll be seen as someone with insight, access, and value to offer.

That is exactly how Andy's Talent Development Hot Seat podcast began. At first, it was just a series of conversations with industry experts. Those conversations expanded Andy's network, grew his reputation, and gave him the confidence to share his own insights through LinkedIn posts, solo podcast episodes, conference hosting, and eventually books. Mike similarly started with blogging and podcasting, which led to speaking engagements, consulting work, and bestselling books. Both of our journeys show that you don't need a massive audience on day one.

Your project doesn't have to be strictly tied to your profession, either; it can be adjacent to your work, or simply something you're passionate about.

Brittany Honor, who works in talent and sales enablement for a major medical device company, started coaching and podcasting on the side. She launched her show, Chess Not Checkers, and regularly shares short insights on Instagram (@honordevelopment). Over time, many of her corporate colleagues have become regular listeners and supporters, strengthening her brand both inside and outside her organization.

Passion projects can lead to great visibility even if not tied directly to your day job, as well. Andy was recently interviewed by professionals running side projects for working parents: one hosted a Substack blog, and the other a podcast, and both had built these outside of their full-time careers. (Check out Decks and Diapers, by Rashi Kakkar, and the Successful Working Parents podcast, by

Anthony Franzese.) Their passion projects expanded their networks, attracted people who could hold meaningful conversations with them, and gave them a public presence that opened unexpected doors.

We should also say that you don't need to commit forever. A short series, like ten podcast episodes or five YouTube interviews, could still raise your profile to a useful extent.

YOU COULD EVEN WRITE A BOOK

Of course, writing a book is a much larger task than posting on LinkedIn, writing a blog, or launching a podcast—but if you've been working for more than ten years, managed a complex project or transformation, or gone through meaningful life experiences, you probably have more than enough stories, lessons, and insights to write your own book.

When Andy wrote his first book in 2020, he did not necessarily see himself as an expert in career development: far from it, in fact. But he *had* just spent years reading, experimenting, and applying different strategies to create a career and business he loved, and over time, he realized he'd developed a practical framework that could help others. That framework became the foundation for his book, which has since led to multiple keynote speaking invitations, corporate training, and new opportunities.

It is important to remember that your book does not need to sell thousands of copies—or even hundreds. Sometimes it only needs to reach the right person. Andy's friend Larry McAlister wrote and self-published a book about his experience leading HR transformations. The book was far from a bestseller, but it ended up in the right hands. When Larry interviewed for a head of HR transformation role, the hiring manager already had his book sitting on her desk. So, what do you think happened? Larry got the job. The book had helped position Larry as the obvious choice for the role.

Writing a book is a pretty meaningful way to crystallize your expertise and open doors you might not even see yet. If you feel the nudge, it might be worth pursuing, because you never know who it could impact.

***

It's easy to underestimate what you have to share. We tend to compare ourselves only to the people ahead of us, and we forget that there are many others who would still benefit from what we already know. You might think, "I only have two years of leadership experience," but there are huge amounts of people with no leadership experience *at all*, and they'd love to learn from you.

Two reminders before you start: first, your content isn't for everyone, so pick one audience and speak to them; trying to please everyone often pleases no one.

Second, critics will always exist. If someone judges you for trying to grow, they were never in your corner anyway. You can't build a meaningful brand while avoiding all criticism, so try to choose growth over approval.

TAKE AND TWEAK THESE TEMPLATES

One of the biggest reasons people hesitate to post content is simple: they don't know what to say. That's where swipe files come in. Swipe files are ready-to-use templates you can customize and make your own. Instead of starting from a blank page every time, you start with a proven structure and then add your voice to it.

The section you're reading now is your shortcut. We've included a handful of prompts, formats, and examples you can use immediately to start posting on LinkedIn or elsewhere without overthinking it. Again, consistent posting with an obvious focus is the most important thing to do.

As you get going, keep these things in mind. Every good post has a point: think about what your reader will take away from it, whether it's a tip, a reminder, or a reflection they'll appreciate. Your posts are about you, but they should also be for your audience, so write with them in mind. The goal is momentum, and the more you post, the easier it gets. Just like a good conversation, your content doesn't have to be polished to be meaningful; it just has to be real.

5 SIMPLE LINKEDIN POST TEMPLATES (YOU CAN USE TODAY)

1. THE QUICK LESSON POST

Format: "This week I learned [lesson] the hard way…" "Here's what happened…" "Here's what I'm taking with me moving forward."

This works especially well when sharing a recent challenge, decision, or mistake.

2. THE BOOK OR ARTICLE REACTION POST

Format: "Just finished reading [title] and one thing jumped out at me…" "[Quote or idea] really stuck with me because…" "If you're in [industry or role], this is worth a read."

This positions you as someone who's learning, and invites conversation.

3. THE ONE-LINER + QUESTION

Format: "[Statement about your industry or experience]." "Agree or disagree?" OR "Curious how others have handled this."

Short, simple, and perfect for engagement.

4. THE BEHIND-THE-SCENES POST

Format: "Here's a small thing we changed at work that made a big difference…" "[Explain the change + why it mattered]" "Sometimes it's the little things."

This is a great way to show impact or culture in a relatable way.

5. THE APPRECIATION POST

Format: "Just wanted to shout out [person or team] for [contribution]." "It reminded me how valuable [quality or behavior] really is." "Thank you for making this a better place to work."

Positive posts like this build goodwill and can subtly show your leadership values.

Important Note: When you first start creating content on LinkedIn (or any other platform), you probably won't get much engagement. That's perfectly normal. You might start to get traction, though, by consistent posting and trying to support others along the way. If you're sharing valuable insights, eventually people will notice and start engaging there. But it often takes a while, so don't get discouraged—just keep trying things and keep going.

You'll find even more swipe files, prompts, and recommendation templates in the workbook at ownyourbrandbook.com. Use them for inspiration, keep them on hand, and pull from them whenever you need a jumpstart.

1. Think of a time when someone said, "I've seen your posts online." What kind of content did they remember—and how did that visibility impact the relationship or opportunity?

2. Think about a recent book, podcast, or article that stood out. What insight did you take from it, and how could sharing that thought publicly reinforce what you want to be known for?

3. Think of a small story from this week—a moment of friction, or perhaps minor epiphany, or change. What was the spark that set it in motion, and what's the simplest takeaway you could share with others?

4. Think about the last time you gave someone advice or encouragement. Were you showing up as the Sage, Sherpa, or Struggler—and how could you use that same voice in your content?

5. Think of a quote or line that hit you in the middle of your workday. Why did it resonate with you, and what part of your real-world experience gives it meaning?

6. Look at your most recent post, or maybe the last one you considered sharing but didn't. Does it reflect the direction you want your brand to go? And, if not, what needs to change?

7. Think of one person in your network you want to influence or support. What challenge are they likely facing, and how can your next post speak directly to that need?

The reality is that everything we've talked about here, from LinkedIn optimization, to content creation, to storytelling, can feel risky if your company doesn't get it.

Maybe you're worried your manager will think you're job hunting; maybe you've heard stories of people getting reprimanded for posting on LinkedIn. Or maybe your company culture treats personal branding like a betrayal (though we hope not).

We get it. But smart companies are starting to realize that when their employees have stronger personal brands, everyone wins.

In the next chapter, we'll change things up and talk directly to companies—and give you the

CHAPTER EIGHT:

THE HIRING TRIFECTA: RESUMES THAT WORK, RECRUITERS WHO HELP YOU, INTERVIEWS THAT LAND THE JOB

As you're building your brand, you might start thinking about landing a new job. But despite all the content you post on LinkedIn and all the tasks AI can automate, landing a role still often comes down to how you look on paper and in-person: your resume and your interview.

Your resume and interview performance will follow you throughout your professional life, but for something so fundamental to career success, most people approach both with outdated advice, generic strategies, and a misunderstanding of how the process actually works.

To get some insider perspective, we spoke with top

recruiters and hiring managers across different industries and company sizes. The gap between what most career advice tells you and what really happens in the hiring process can be massive. If you're serious about building your personal brand and advancing your career, let's get into it.

REAL TALK: THE HIRING PROCESS ISN'T ALWAYS FAIR

First, let's set realistic expectations. The hiring process isn't always logical, fair, or based purely on qualifications. Knowing this up-front will save you frustration and help you approach job searching more pragmatically.

Case in point: one of our sources told us about a company that was hiring for a director of supply chain role and interviewed two candidates. Marcus had everything on paper: all the right experience, certifications, and background that the job description called for. But during the interview process, something felt "off" about how he might fit into the culture of the company.

The second candidate, Ben, had about 90% of the desired qualifications but seemed like he would have better chemistry with the team. The hiring team genuinely liked him more, but he didn't check every box on their requirements list. The company ended up hiring Marcus, the guy who *wasn't* a cultural fit, at $180,000.

The interesting part is that six months later, when the company asked if Ben happened to still be available and he was (though he could easily have taken another job during that time), the company jumped at the opportunity and finally hired him. They offered him a lower-level position for $150,000, $30,000 less than Marcus's salary.

This wasn't the result of some brilliant long-term strategy of theirs: the company had been changing requirements and second-guessing themselves for months, and when they realized Ben was still on the market, they saw their chance to fix their earlier mistake without admitting they'd made one.

Over time, they systematically pushed out Marcus, essentially demoting him to report to Ben, who eventually got promoted to the director role they'd both originally interviewed for. Marcus eventually resigned (understandably).

The whole process took over a year to properly fill the position because the company had kept wavering through their own indecision. In the end, they got lucky. The person with 90% of the qualifications but great energy beat the person with 100% of the qualifications who couldn't connect with the team. It just took a messy, expensive detour to get there.

This is how the hiring game can play out. Companies aren't always perfect in their strategy and implementation: they are, after all, led by humans. Sometimes they find their way to the right outcome through a combination of luck, persistence, and candidates who are still available when opportunity strikes again.

We know it's hard, but don't take rejection personally

when the process itself is often messy and inconsistent. Understanding these realities means approaching the process thoughtfully. Let's break down exactly how hiring works so you can position yourself effectively at each stage.

HOW THE HIRING PROCESS REALLY WORKS

Let's first look at the key players to be aware of:

- **The Recruiter** is your first point of contact. Their job is to source and filter candidates, conduct early screenings, and keep communication flowing between you and the hiring team.

- **The Hiring Manager** is the decision-maker. They define what they're looking for, interview finalists, and ultimately choose who gets hired.

- **HR or People Operations** coordinates the process but focuses more on offer letters, background checks, and onboarding logistics.

Now let's take a bird's-eye view at how all this works at most mid-to-large companies with structured HR departments:

1. **The Job Gets Posted:** A hiring manager (the person who would be your boss) identifies a need for a new team member. They work with HR to create or update a job description, then post it on company websites, job boards like LinkedIn or Indeed, or share it

through internal referrals.

2. **Your Application Goes Into the System:** When you submit your resume and cover letter through an online portal, it gets processed by an Applicant Tracking System (ATS). This software scans your resume for keywords and formatting before any human sees it. Please note that not all companies use ATS keyword filters to filter candidates. Many smaller companies, startups, and even some larger organizations with less automated recruitment processes will still have a human skim every resume, even if the ATS flags potential issues.

3. **The Recruiter Screen:** If your resume stands out, a recruiter from HR or a third-party agency conducts an initial screen. This is usually a short phone call lasting 15-30 minutes to confirm basic qualifications, salary expectations, availability, and genuine interest in the role.

4. **Hiring Manager Review:** The hiring manager reviews resumes and recommendations from the recruiter. If they're interested, you move to the formal interview stage.

5. **Multiple Interview Rounds:** Most companies conduct several interviews. The first round is typically a video or phone interview with the hiring manager or a team member. The second round often involves meeting multiple stakeholders like team members

or cross-functional peers. The final round sometimes includes a task, presentation, or panel interview and may involve senior leadership.

6. **References and Background Check:** If you're the top candidate, companies can ask for professional references and may conduct background checks or employment verification.

7. **Offer and Negotiation:** HR, the recruiter, or sometimes the hiring manager extends an offer, often verbally first, then in writing. This is when you can negotiate salary, benefits, or start date.

WRITING A WINNING RESUME: SCALE, SCOPE, AND IMPACT

Most resumes are subpar; no sense beating around the bush on that. It's not because the people writing them lack experience or qualifications, but usually because they misunderstand what a resume is supposed to do. Your resume isn't your life story: it's a marketing document designed to get your foot in the door for a specific opportunity.

With all the software, templates, and AI available today, resumes can be easier to write and format than ever before—but that doesn't mean they're informative, insightful, or tell a compelling story about who you are and what you can accomplish.

To go deeper on this, let's revisit our friend Henry Jeong (henryjeong.com) from Chapter 4. After years of screening resumes at major retail chains, food companies, and various startups, Henry recommends a "Scale, Scope, and Impact" framework for your resume.

Henry regularly sees resumes that are pages long, filled with impressive company names and great schools, but difficult to scan or understand. "I don't know what they want," he explains about these types of resumes. "If I can't figure out who someone is in 30 seconds, I'm moving on to the next one."

The problem is that many people write their resumes like job descriptions. They list everything they were responsible for without giving any indication of what they really accomplished or the impact they made.

A recruiter really wants to know how you performed in a role differently than someone else would have. The "Scale, Scope, and Impact" framework changes how you present your experience:

- **Scale:** What was the size of the project, team, or budget you worked with?

- **Scope:** What was the breadth of your responsibilities or the complexity of the work?

- **Impact:** What measurable results did you achieve?

Here's an example of the difference this makes:

- **Before:** "Managed events for the company."
- **After:** "Coordinated 50+ interdepartmental meetings monthly for 3 senior executives, streamlining communication processes that reduced project delays by 25% and improved cross-team collaboration metrics."

Same person, same job, but completely different story. The first version is generic and forgettable. It could describe anyone in any company doing any kind of event work. The second version makes you think, "How did they do that?" instead of "So does everyone else."

This is also why understanding keywords can be so helpful. A recruiter is often looking for specific terms, specific years of experience, and specific types of companies or roles in your background. Instead of saying you "tested client campaigns," use "A/B tested client campaigns"—the industry-specific term that recruiters are probably searching for.

For marketing roles, recruiters look for terms like "conversion optimization," "marketing automation," and "customer acquisition cost." For recruiting positions, they search for "ATS systems," "LinkedIn recruiter," "sourcing," "high volume recruitment," and "full cycle recruitment."

These are the exact terms that come up in intake conversations with hiring managers. When a hiring manager tells a recruiter they need someone with experience in "conversion optimization," that's the keyword they put into the system. If your resume says "improving sales results" instead, you might not show up in their search results, even though you have the exact experience they want.

To identify your keywords, analyze 5-10 job descriptions in your target field. What industry-specific terms appear repeatedly? Make sure these terms appear naturally in your resume summary and throughout your experience descriptions.

THE PROFESSIONAL SUMMARY GAME-CHANGER

The next vital element is how you open your resume. The top of a resume is prime real estate that most people waste with generic objective statements or outdated summaries. There are two formats that actually work: the statement format and the skills-based format.

The statement format reads like a powerful introduction that tells your story in a few sentences:

- Strategic, solutions-focused executive assistant with 10+ years of experience supporting C-level executives in fast-paced environments, specializing in process optimization and cross-functional team coordination.

The skills-based format lists industry-specific keywords that recruiters are searching for:

- Talent Management • Data Analysis •

Full-Cycle Recruitment • ATS Optimization •
High-Volume Hiring • Workforce Planning

If you're trying to break into a new field or level, use skills; if you're established and want to tell your story, use the statement. Whatever you do, make sure the most important information is at the top since that's what gets scanned first.

THE TEN-YEAR GUIDELINE FOR RESUMES

Generally, anything older than ten years should be cut from your resume. Typically, recruiters don't need to know what you did ten years ago when they're trying to fill a role today.

The exception is that if you have highly relevant experience that directly relates to the specific role you're applying for, you can include it. Some industries—like academia, government, or roles requiring deep technical expertise—might value longer career histories where earlier experience shows important qualifications.

This ten-year guideline forces you to focus on your most relevant, recent experience and keeps your resume to the one- or two-page maximum that actually gets read. For most professionals, one page works for entry to mid-level roles, while two pages is appropriate for senior positions. Be selective and make sure your updates add real value to your resume rather than just filling space.

RECRUITERS ARE YOUR FIRST ADVOCATE

Most people think recruiters are gatekeepers trying to keep them out. In reality, recruiters are measured on successful placements, which means they want you to succeed.

The process begins when a recruiter sits down with the hiring manager to understand what they're looking for. This isn't always straightforward. Hiring managers say they want A, B, and C, which informs the job description, but that's not what they always really want. For example, they might want someone with "strong leadership skills" but what they really mean is someone who can manage up to difficult executives. Or they'll ask for "communication skills" when what they need is someone who can translate technical concepts for non-technical stakeholders.

The job description you see posted online is often generic and incomplete. The real requirements come from what recruiters call the "intake conversation," and that's what drives the keyword searches and screening criteria. Smart recruiters probe deeper by asking questions like:

- Is this a new role or replacing someone? If replacing someone, what happened?

- What are the must-haves versus nice-to-haves?

- What will be the most challenging aspects of this role?

- If you could have the ideal person in this role, what would that look like?

- What do you definitely *not* want to see in a candidate?

Important note: These are not questions you should ask during your interview. These are thought exercises to help you understand what the company really needs. With the question, "What's the career path for this person?" you could reverse-engineer it to think: "What is the career path for this role I'm applying for?" If you're applying for a marketing coordinator position, is this a role that typically leads to marketing manager, or is it more of a specialized track?

Understanding these realities helps you make smarter career decisions. You're trying to get hired, sure, but you're also evaluating whether this role moves you toward where you actually want to go.

When recruiters find a good candidate, they can become your strongest advocates. Since your success is their success, the best ones can be open to giving you feedback, prepping you for interviews, and help you understand what a hiring manager is really looking for.

The candidates who get results treat recruiters like allies. They respond quickly, ask thoughtful questions, and remember that being pleasant to interact with goes a long way, especially when recruiters are juggling multiple candidates for the same role.

Remember that smart recruiters go beyond today's

needs and try to build relationships for the future. Henry told us, "I've placed people who didn't get the first job they interviewed for with me: I remembered them, and when the right role came along, I reached out."

We recommend starting by connecting with 3-5 recruiters who specialize in your field on LinkedIn. Engage with their content, share their posts when relevant, and be a real person they actually want to help. Stay on their radar, be genuinely grateful for their time, and keep them posted on successes in your career. When the perfect opportunity opens up, you want to be the first person they think of.

INTERVIEW EXCELLENCE: FRAMEWORKS THAT ACTUALLY WORK

If your resume gets you to the interview stage, congratulations! You've already beaten most of the competition. Now, what do you do to prepare for it?

There are tons of generic interview questions you can find online: "Tell me about yourself," "What's your greatest weakness," "Where do you see yourself in five years," "Tell me about a time you failed," "Why do you want this job?" You should definitely prepare for these, but having good answers isn't enough.

Instead of trying to memorize perfect responses to every possible question, it's better to use frameworks that help you organize your thoughts and deliver clear, compelling answers.

Most interview questions fall into three basic categories: questions about your past experience, questions about how you'd handle future situations, and questions about your background and motivations. Having a reliable framework for each type means you'll never be caught off guard, even when they throw you a curveball.

The frameworks below are thinking tools that help you stay focused and tell complete stories that actually answer what the interviewer is looking for. Let's break down three effective approaches:

STAR Framework: Use for behavioral questions

- **When you hear:** "Tell me about a time when…" or "Give me an example of…"
- **Best for:** Past experience and situation-based questions

IDEAL Framework: Use for situational and problem-solving questions

- **When you hear:** "How would you handle…" or "What would you do if…"
- **Best for:** Hypothetical scenarios and technical problem-solving

HERO Framework: Use for background and motivation questions

- **When you hear:** "Tell me about yourself" or "Why do you want this job?"

- **Best for:** Career story and motivation questions

THE STAR FRAMEWORK

When you hear "tell me about a time when..." your brain might race through every work memory you've ever had. Here's where STAR saves you from having to scramble like that:

- **Situation:** Set the scene—what was happening?

- **Task:** What did you need to accomplish?

- **Action:** What did you actually do about it?

- **Result:** How did it turn out?

Let's say they ask about a time you failed. Instead of panicking or giving a vague non-answer, you might say something like:

- "I was managing a cross-functional team launch for a new client onboarding system (situation). My role was to coordinate between IT, customer success, and sales to ensure we delivered on time and hit our user adoption targets (task). I implemented daily standups and milestone tracking, but about halfway through, I realized our original success metrics were too narrow—we were only measuring system functionality, not actual user experience (action). So I expanded our testing to include real customer scenarios and added a feedback loop with the customer success team. As a result, we launched one week later than planned, but achieved 40% higher user adoption than any previous rollout (result). That experience taught me to define success more holistically from the start, and I now always include end-user experience metrics in my initial project planning."

STAR keeps you from rambling for five minutes or giving a three-word answer that leaves the interviewer wondering what you actually do at work.

THE IDEAL FRAMEWORK

When interviewers ask "What would you do if…" they're testing how you think through problems instead of whether you have the one "right" answer. The Ideal framework helps you sound thoughtful and methodical:

- **Issue:** What's the core problem you're dealing with?

- **Direction:** Where are you trying to get to?

- **Explore:** What are your options here?

- **Action:** What's your best move?

- **Learn:** How would you make sure it worked?

This works great for questions like "What would you do if you realized a project was off-track?" or "How would you handle conflicting priorities from two different stake-holders?" Here's how it might sound:

- "If I realized a key team member was consistently missing deliverables because they seemed over-whelmed (issue), my goal would be understand-ing what's really going on and getting them back on track without damaging team morale (direc-tion). I'd consider whether it's a workload prob-lem, a skills gap, personal issues, or unclear expec-tations—and I'd weigh options like redistributing tasks, providing additional training, or having a one-on-one conversation (explore). I'd start with a private conversation to understand their per-spective, then work together on a realistic plan to catch up while adjusting their workload if need-ed (action). I'd schedule weekly check-ins for the next month to make sure the solution is actually working and watch for early warning signs with other team members (learn)."

The framework shows you can break down complex problems systematically instead of just throwing solutions at the wall. Even if your specific approach isn't exactly what they'd do, they can see how you think.

THE HERO FRAMEWORK

"Tell me about yourself" is probably the most dread-ed interview question because it's so open-ended. The HERO framework gives you a roadmap that feels natural while hitting all the points they actually care about:

- **History:** Your career story in 30 seconds or less
- **Expertise:** What you're genuinely good at
- **Reasons:** Why you want this specific job
- **Objective:** Where you're headed next

This handles classics like "Why do you want to work here?" and "Why should we hire you?" without sounding like you memorized a script. Here's how it can flow:

- "I've spent six years in HR operations, mostly with fast-growing companies that needed solid processes fast (**history**). I'm really good at stream-lining onboarding and building training programs that actually keep people around (**expertise**). What draws me to your team is your reputation for genuinely investing in employees—that's exactly the kind of culture I love helping build (**reasons**). I'm looking to take on more strategic HR work and eventually move into a management role as teams scale (**objective**)."

This response succinctly covers everything they need to know and ends with where you want to go.

***

Beyond these frameworks, you'll encounter other questions that each serve a specific purpose:

Culture Fit Questions: These might seem random, but they're designed to see if you'll mesh with the company's values and environment. For example, Whole Foods might ask candidates, "If I were coming over for dinner, what would you make for me?" It seems strange at first, but they want to see if you understand their food-focused culture and can think on your feet in a friendly, personal way.

Problem-Solving Questions: You might get seemingly bizarre questions like "If you had an elephant that you can't sell and can't give away, what would you do with it?" These aren't exactly riddles with right answers; it's that interviewers want to see your thought process, creativity, and how you approach unexpected challenges.

Self-Assessment Questions: "If you had to describe yourself as a leader in three words, what would they be?" This is about self-awareness and whether you can articulate your leadership style clearly and confidently.

Managing Up Questions: "Tell me about a time you provided constructive feedback to a manager" tests whether you can navigate workplace hierarchies diplomatically and communicate effectively with authority figures.

The key is recognizing that these questions aren't tests of your knowledge but rather windows into how you think, communicate, and would fit into their specific work environment.

A FEW OTHER ESSENTIAL INTERVIEW GUIDELINES

Keep responses short: When you have just 30 minutes to an hour for an interview, you need to make every minute count. If you're taking five minutes to answer a simple question, you'll lose people. Keep your answers to two to three minutes maximum. If the interviewer wants more detail, they'll ask follow-up questions.

Understand the real question they're asking: Questions aren't asking what you think they're asking. When someone asks about your greatest weakness or a time you failed, they're not looking for a confession. They're asking: "Are you self-aware enough to identify areas for improvement, and do you take action to address them?"

When finished, stop talking: Here's a crucial tip most candidates miss: when you finish answering, stop talking. Most candidates panic in silence and try to fill it with additional rambling, but silence is golden. It makes you look confident and in-control. It's extremely important. Let the interviewer guide what's next.

WHEN IT'S YOUR TURN TO ASK QUESTIONS

At the end of some interviews, you'll hear: "Do you have any questions for us?" Most people ask generic questions or say they don't have any. Big mistake.

This is your opportunity to demonstrate strategic thinking and genuine interest in the role. More importantly, it's your chance to gather intelligence about what you're really walking into. Here are some effective questions you can ask:

- **"What does success look like in this role after six months? After a year?"** This shows you're thinking about performance and gives you concrete goals to reference if you get the job.

- **"What's your management style?"** Ask this directly to your potential manager to understand how they operate.

- **"If you could change one thing about the culture here, what would it be?"** Ask this to everyone you meet, then compare answers. Consistency is good; contradictions are red flags.

- **"What do you anticipate being the most challenging aspects of this role in the first six months?"** This is a diplomatic way to ask, "What problems am I walking into?"

- **"I saw that the company recently [launched X product/opened Y location/announced Z partnership]. How is that affecting this department?"** This demonstrates you've researched the company and are thinking strategically.

The questions you ask should feel natural and conversational, not like you're reading from a list. Pick three to five questions that genuinely interest you and fit the flow of your conversation. This is your chance to interview them as much as they're interviewing you.

WHAT ABOUT SENIOR ROLES?

The more senior the role, the less likely it is to be filled through a traditional process. Sometimes they come internally through a mentor or sponsor recommending someone for a higher role, like May Busch's story in Chapter 3. In other instances, roles are filled through networking or executive search firms rather than online applications.

When companies are paying substantial placement fees for senior roles—typically 25-33% of first-year salary through retained search firms—they expect a very different caliber of candidate and process. For executive roles with $300,000+ salaries, these fees can reach $100,000 or more, but even director-level positions involve significant investment from companies. At this level, your personal brand and professional reputation become more important than your resume.

Executive search firms maintain networks of pre-vetted candidates. They know who's doing what at which companies, who might be ready for a change, and who has the specific background and personality fit for different types of roles. Getting on their radar requires the kind of visibility and relationship-building we've discussed throughout this book.

As at the end of our other chapters, below are the key actions from this chapter. As we've noted, these exercises are also in our workbook, available at ownyourbrandbook.com.

1. **Audit your resume** using the Scale, Scope, and Impact framework. For each role, identify: What was the scale of your work? What was the scope of your responsibilities? What measurable impact did you achieve?

2. **Research keywords** by analyzing 5-10 job descriptions in your target field. What industry-specific terms appear repeatedly? Make sure these appear naturally in your resume.

3. **Practice your frameworks:** Prepare STAR responses for behavioral questions, IDEAL responses for situational questions, and your HERO pitch for "Tell me about yourself."

4. **Develop strategic interview questions** that reveal the real situation you'd be walking into.

5. **Connect with 3-5 recruiters** in your field on LinkedIn and engage thoughtfully with their content.

6. **Reverse-engineer target roles** by thinking through: Is this a growth opportunity or a problem situation? Where does this position typically lead, and does this align with where I want to go?

7. **Rewrite your professional summary** using either the statement format (if you're established) or skills-based format (if you're breaking into a new field or level).

Remember, you're trying to go beyond "just getting any job" to landing opportunities that align with your values, leverage your strengths, and move you toward your career objectives.

But what happens after you land that role? The smartest companies today understand that your personal brand doesn't stop at the office door; the most forward-thinking organizations are actively encouraging employees to build them, and they're seeing remarkable results because of it.

In the next chapter, we'll explore how progressive companies are turning their employees into brand ambassadors, why this trend is accelerating, and what it means for your career strategy.

CHAPTER NINE:
DEAR COMPANIES, YOUR PEOPLE ARE YOUR BRAND

Back in 2017, I (Andy) was working for a consulting firm while quietly starting to explore new career possibilities. I launched a podcast and began posting more on LinkedIn to share ideas and expand my network. I felt like I had a lot to share with the world and that there was potential to add value to the firm as well. At one point I even suggested I start a new podcast to showcase the work we were doing.

Unfortunately I was met with more skepticism and concern than support. Eventually I was told that several leaders were worried about my dedication to the firm and my job. The subtext was clear: they saw my personal branding efforts as a distraction from "real work." wss

The skepticism only grew over time. Other leaders started questioning how I was spending my time and dismissed my ideas about leveraging what I was learning to help the firm grow. To them, building a personal brand

169

OWN YOUR BRAND, OWN YOUR CAREER

meant I was preparing an exit strategy rather than adding value to the organization.

I know I wasn't alone. Back then, many companies still saw personal branding as a distraction or red flag. I've heard countless stories from professionals who were afraid to even comment on a LinkedIn post, worried their employer might see their activity and think they were looking for a new job. I've certainly heard stories of people being reprimanded or even terminated for building a presence online or starting a side business.

This old-school thinking still exists in many organizations. More recently, a friend told me she was reprimanded by company executives because they discovered her side hustle: a small cohort program for job-seekers. She was allowed to keep running it, but she was forbidden from posting about it on LinkedIn. Ouch!

To me, this is a big missed opportunity and a fundamental misunderstanding of how value is created in today's economy. What if they embraced and supported her efforts and some of those job seekers took roles at the company? Would it be a distraction or a boost to the business?

Thankfully, things are starting to change. Forward-thinking organizations are starting to realize that when employees show up with better focus, more confidence, and more industry connections—and start sharing their expertise with the world—everyone benefits.

Eventually, I left that consulting firm and joined a more progressive organization (shout out to Advantage

Performance Group) that supported my content creation efforts and even helped me launch my second podcast. I have to say that it was quite a difference. I expanded my network, landed speaking opportunities, built new business relationships, and became more valuable in the talent development space—and all of this while creating measurable value for a firm that was supporting my growth.

A few years later, the founder of the original firm I worked for reached out to me for advice on building a presence on LinkedIn. After years of neglecting the platform, he realized it was going to matter significantly in the next phase of his career. It's funny how things evolved.

One of my favorite examples of this is my friend Darren McKee. In 2020, Darren started posting daily on LinkedIn about his sales career, sharing successes, lessons, and setbacks. His personal brand translated directly into business results: a new startup position, explosive company growth through his increased sales and visibility, and a side business teaching LinkedIn growth.

That side business eventually became his full-time venture, but not before his social selling approach generated massive results for his employer, including their eventual acquisition.

Today, Darren advocates for personal branding for startups and salespeople to create win-win scenarios for employees and employers. His success came from understanding what more companies are recognizing: people trust *people* more than they do brands.

When I asked Darren about the importance of companies supporting their people in sharing content, he said, "employees are your company's voice, so let them speak! I'm not talking about leadership, I'm talking about everyone from emerging leaders to the c-suite. Employee Generated Content (EGC) is non-negotiable in the current era—it screams psychological safety and trust, which is what we all want at the end of the day. Empower your employee's voices and watch what happens to them individually and your organization as a whole."

If you work in sales or run a startup, you need to follow Darren on LinkedIn.

THE WAR FOR TALENT

Consider this parallel: you're often more likely to see a movie or try a restaurant because a friend recommended it than because you saw an ad. The same psychology applies to career decisions. A team photo with a genuine caption like "Grateful to work with this crew every day" often does more to boost a company's reputation than any paid campaign declaring "We're a great place to work."

This change in how trust is built matters enormously because companies have begun to fight an increasingly difficult battle for talent.

Despite all the headlines about AI displacing jobs, the bigger challenge in many industries is finding qualified people to fill critical roles. According to ManpowerGroup's 2024 Global Talent Shortage Survey, 75% of employers globally reported difficulty filling positions.

Korn Ferry's "The Future of Work" report projects an even starker scenario: by 2030, more than 85 million jobs could go unfilled due to a lack of qualified candidates. This represents an estimated $8.5 trillion gap in lost revenue and productivity.

Companies understand these stakes and pour significant resources into employer branding, competing to land on lists like Fortune's "100 Best Companies to Work For." Some rankings rely on employee feedback (like Glassdoor or Indeed), while others like Fortune involve extensive applications.

Not to say anything is inherently wrong with these efforts, but they're majoring in the minors while minoring in the majors, to use a baseball metaphor. When employees share genuine experiences about their work, culture, and growth, it results in a better brand and more business. So how do companies make this shift?

A MAJOR OPPORTUNITY FOR COMPANIES

As we interviewed experts and researched this topic, it became more and more obvious that supporting employees and leaders in building their brands and sharing content online was a huge missed opportunity for so many companies.

Jessica Lorimer, a successful sales consultant and coach who has been working with organizations and professionals across different industries for more than 10 years (and who is Andy's personal sales coach), said that it's quite amazing how much companies spend on branding and recruiting while their best asset is often existing employees sharing positive stories. She said, "It's actually much easier to generate the best candidates inside companies by getting your own employees to advocate for how great the company is, and when employees post about good experiences, achievements, or culture, it signals to others that the company is a great place to work. That boosts the company's **credibility, visibility, and relevance** in a competitive landscape." This sounds like a huge opportunity.

Liam Darmody, the LinkedIn expert and personal brand strategist who formerly worked in employer branding for a small company, said, "When you give your employees the ability—and the encouragement—to go out and share their voice with their network on a regular basis, they're automatically attracting eyeballs to your brand. That can be a very powerful thing."

This improves the employer brand, improves recruiting by building trust with potential candidates, and even improves employee loyalty. It's not an easy change to make if the company has historically been against people sharing content online, but the change *can* be made and lead to strong results for the company.

THE THREE-STAGE COMPANY EVOLUTION

In our experience, organizations typically progress through three distinct stages in their approach to employee personal branding:

- **Stage 1: Restriction** - These companies maintain "no social media" policies, viewing employee online presence as a potential liability. They worry that employees will say something inappropriate or use their platform to job hunt. We've seen employee handbooks that discourage posting about work or mentioning the company on social media. As a result, their talent is invisible online while competitors showcase their team's expertise.

- **Stage 2: Permission** - Companies at this stage have loosened restrictions but offer no support. Their unofficial policy is "You can post, but don't mention the company." Employees feel allowed to build personal brands but must separate their professional identity from their employer. Some companies might be cool with LinkedIn posting but request that employees avoid mentioning specific projects or company culture, unless they're sharing official company content. This creates an artificial divide that can limit both individual and organizational growth.

- **Stage 3: Partnership** - Forward-thinking organizations actively collaborate with employees to create content that showcases both individual expertise and company culture. These companies recognize that employee success and company success are interconnected.

Dr. Keith Keating is a great example of the partnership approach. As Chief Learning Officer of BDO Canada, he's published two books: *The Trusted Learning Advisor* and *Hidden Talent*. When I asked Keith how his employer views his writing and thought leadership activities, he picked up his latest book and showed me the company logo prominently displayed on the cover.

BDO not only approves of his activities: they champion them. Keith's latest book features a detailed case study about the company, creating a great illustration of their culture and capabilities. The marketing team promotes his speaking engagements, leadership amplifies his LinkedIn posts, and at every conference or podcast, he's introduced as both a respected expert and a proud BDO leader. "It's already paying off with greater attention, credibility, and opportunities for both me and the firm," Keith told me. "It's proof that when personal brand and company brand work in harmony, it fuels our journey to being a Top Tier firm — and everyone benefits from the momentum."

For more on this, check out Andy's interview with Keith on the Talent Development Hot Seat podcast.

This isn't a revolutionary concept. Universities have traditionally encouraged professors to publish research because it elevates the entire institution's reputation. When a Stanford professor publishes groundbreaking research, it reflects positively on Stanford's academic standing. Professional services firms like Deloitte, Ernst & Young, PWC, and McKinsey have built their reputations partly on the thought leadership their partners produce.

Tech companies have also embraced this approach for years. Guy Kawasaki's relationship with Apple in the 1980s is a great example. When Kawasaki joined Apple in 1983, he stepped into a role that barely existed in tech before: chief evangelist. His mission was convincing third-party developers and hardware makers to build for the Macintosh platform, even though the Mac had no installed user base. It was a role that required confidence, enthusiasm, and personal credibility more than traditional sales tactics.

Kawasaki spoke at conferences, wrote for major tech magazines, and built relationships with the developer community. His personal credibility became a bridge between Apple and the broader tech world. He helped popularize the term "evangelist" in technology marketing, turning it into a model that countless companies would later emulate.

In 1995, when Apple needed to reconnect with its core users, he returned as an Apple Fellow. His role was helping reignite the Macintosh community and brand. In practice, Apple turned Kawasaki into a brand ambassador long before today's practice of hiring external influencers. They understood that their own people could be their most authentic advocates.

Through that process, Kawasaki gained fame that benefited him in his career and at the same time, Apple's brand grew and the company gained billions of dollars in shareholder value.

Now, companies across all industries are discovering

that when employees speak publicly about their work, it makes the organization more visible, more attractive, and more trusted by both potential talent and customers. Andy's friend, Amit Parmer, founder and CEO of Cliquify, which helps companies amplify employer branding through employee stories, told us that employee-shared content generates *eight times* more engagement than company-posted content. It's clear that people instinctively trust personal perspectives over corporate messaging.

Parmer says his clients have driven over 350,000 people to apply for jobs through employer-branded stories shared by employees. That's the equivalent of $3–4 million in LinkedIn advertising spending, or roughly $200–300 in value per post.

The implications are pretty big. If companies actively encouraged and supported employees in sharing branded content, the return on investment would far outweigh the risk of losing members who discover new passions along the way.

THE FOUR TYPES OF ORGANIZATIONAL RESISTANCE

All this sounds great, but we need to acknowledge that most organizations haven't evolved to a Stage 3 partnership. In our experience, organizational pushback against employee personal branding seems to fall into four categories:

1. **Control Concerns:** These organizations worry about message consistency and brand protection. They want to control every external communication to ensure it aligns with official messaging. The underlying fear: "What if employees say something that contradicts our marketing or makes us look bad?"

2. **Competitive Fears:** Companies in this category worry that employees building personal brands will become more attractive to competitors. They see external networking and thought leadership as preparation for departure. The underlying fear: "What if we invest in developing their personal brand and they leave for a competitor?"

3. **Distraction Anxieties:** These employers view any time spent on personal branding activities as time stolen from "real work." They see posting on LinkedIn, writing articles, or attending networking events as productivity drains. The underlying fear: "How do we know they're not just building their personal business on company time?"

4. **Cultural Misalignment:** Some organizations simply haven't evolved their culture to embrace individual thought leadership. They may operate from old models where company loyalty meant keeping your head down and not drawing external attention. The underlying fear: "This isn't how we've always done things and change feels risky."

Wherever you sit on the org chart, you can work with these concerns instead of fighting against them. Here's what's helped me and the professionals I've worked with navigate this territory:

START WITH SMALL, SPECIFIC REQUESTS.

Instead of requesting broad permission to "build your personal brand" (which sounds vague and potentially threatening), get approval for specific activities:

- "I'd like to share a short post about the project our team just completed, highlighting how our approach helped the client succeed. I'll run the draft by you first to make sure it aligns with our messaging."

- Or try: "I want to make sure I'm representing our company well online. Could we establish some guidelines for how I can share our team's successes on LinkedIn while staying aligned with our brand standards?"

These requests feel collaborative rather than confrontational. You're asking for partnership instead of permission to go rogue.

SHOW THEM THE BUSINESS VALUE.

If your boss is worried about competition, demonstrate that your activities actually create value. Start tracking any business development leads, partnership opportunities, or talent referrals that result from your networking and content creation, and create a simple monthly report showing the business impact:

- "Three prospects mentioned they follow my LinkedIn content when they reached out for sales conversations"

- "Two qualified candidates applied for our open positions after seeing my posts about our company culture"

- "This industry association invited me to speak at their conference, where I can represent our company to 200+ potential clients"

When you present this data, try something like: "I've been tracking the business impact of my LinkedIn activities and I wanted to share some results with you. Would you be interested in seeing how my external networking is generating leads and referrals for our team?"

ADDRESS THE PERFORMANCE QUESTION HEAD-ON.

If leadership is concerned about your focus, be transparent about your time investment: "I spend 15 minutes before work each day engaging on LinkedIn and post content during lunch breaks. I attend one networking event per month, always outside work hours, and I write articles on weekends—though I often incorporate insights that benefit our client work."

Or ask: "I want to be transparent about the time I'm

investing in professional development activities and how I'm ensuring they don't interfere with my work responsibilities. Can we discuss expectations and boundaries?"

You might also add that spending time on LinkedIn is a great way to keep up with the latest trends and learn about how people are using different tools, which could be really valuable to you and your team.

TRY THE PILOT PROJECT APPROACH.

One of the most effective strategies I've seen is proposing a 90-day experiment:

- "I'd like to propose a trial run where I share insights about our industry and our team's work on LinkedIn, with your approval on all content. At the end of 90 days, let's evaluate whether this activity generated any measurable business value or positive exposure for our company. If it doesn't show results, I'll scale back. If it does, we can discuss expanding the approach."

Don't try to change organizational culture single-handedly. Instead, identify and develop relationships with internal advocates who can help vouch for your approach. Look for progressive managers who already understand the value of employee thought leadership, HR leaders focused on talent attraction and retention, marketing colleagues who understand content creation and brand building, sales team members who appreciate the value of personal networking, and fellow employees who are also interested in professional development. These allies can help you build momentum and demonstrate that personal branding is a strategic advantage for the entire organization.

Whatever approach you take, consistently measure and communicate the business value your personal branding activities create. Track metrics like:

- **Lead generation:** Prospects who mention seeing your content

- **Talent attraction:** Qualified candidates who cite your posts as factors in their interest

- **Speaking opportunities:** Invitations to represent the company at events

- **Media coverage:** Journalists who contact you for expert commentary

- **Partnership opportunities:** Other organizations interested in collaboration

- **Employee engagement:** Colleagues who start following your example

Sometimes, despite your best efforts, the organization just isn't ready. That's frustrating, but remember that company policies and cultures can evolve. You're planting seeds that might not sprout immediately but could bloom when the timing is right. In the meantime, there's one group that can't afford to wait to embrace personal branding: leaders themselves.

LEADERS: TOP TALENT IS WATCHING, EVEN WHEN THEY'RE NOT LOOKING

Leaders play a far bigger role in talent attraction and retention than most realize. In many organizations, recruiting is seen as HR's responsibility. The truth is, however, that exceptional employees join leaders just as much (or more) than companies.

This is especially critical in today's market, where top talent is increasingly difficult to reach through traditional channels. A recent Gartner study revealed that high-performing professionals are the least likely to respond to recruiter outreach. They're not scrolling job boards or replying to LinkedIn messages from strangers.

So how do you capture their attention? You show up authentically in the spaces where they're already engaged: within their professional networks. Again: people follow people. On platforms like LinkedIn, personal profiles consistently outperform company pages in both reach and engagement. This means if you're a leader, your voice might be your company's most valuable recruiting asset.

We covered LinkedIn tactics for individual professionals in Chapter 6, but now we're talking about something different: how leaders can use these same principles to build their leadership brand and attract top talent to their organizations.

Travis Dommert (travisdommert.com), a talent executive and leadership speaker, puts it well: "The single biggest risk in the war for talent is a bad manager. The single most powerful weapon in the war for talent is an attractive manager." When someone develops a reputation as an exceptional leader, others naturally want to work for them. That reputation is built through meaningful interactions within the organization and, increasingly, through the content and conversations leaders share publicly.

Travis identifies three essential elements for leaders building effective personal brands: clear focus, consistency, and constancy.

1. **Clear focus** means understanding who you are, what you stand for, and what brand you want to project. This includes your strengths, what makes you unique, the value you bring to others, your core values, and what genuinely energizes you. A simple framework Travis uses with leaders is: "I love using [my talents or insights] to help [my audience] experience or achieve [specific outcome]."

2. **Consistency** means showing up in alignment with your brand every day and maintaining a regular online presence. This might look like engaging on LinkedIn daily and publishing content at least weekly or monthly, depending on your capacity and goals.

3. **Constancy** refers to maintaining that strong brand over time so you can realize the long-term benefits for both yourself and your organization.

Here's how to put this into action right now:

- **This week:** Update your LinkedIn headline to include your leadership philosophy. Instead of "VP of Operations at Company X," try something like "VP of Operations helping manufacturing teams optimize efficiency while maintaining safety standards."

- **This month:** Share one post about your team's recent success, giving specific credit to team members and explaining your role in supporting their achievement.

- **This quarter:** Engage with five industry professionals' content weekly by leaving thoughtful comments that add value to the conversation.

When leaders regularly share what they're learning, they build visibility and trust. It signals to potential talent: "Here's how we operate. Here's what we believe. Here are the kind of people we want to grow with." As leaders expand their networks and share valuable content, they naturally attract attention from industry professionals who start thinking, "I wonder what it would be like to work there?"

And this is not just for mid-level managers. Some of the best CEOs and executives are realizing the value of sharing content online to build their brands and the brands of their companies. One great example is Hal Lawton, who is the CEO of Tractor Supply Company. Hal shares regularly on LinkedIn about his company's

DEAR COMPANIES, YOUR PEOPLE ARE YOUR BRAND

events and his visits to different stores and districts. As a result, he has over 46,000 followers on LinkedIn and has built a brand as a strong leader at an attractive company. If you were looking for a job, would you rather work under a mysterious CEO who hides in the boardroom and rarely shares anything, or one who is seemingly out there working on the front-line with the people and talking about it regularly? We prefer the latter, and bet most others do as well.

Companies winning the war for talent have figured out something important: one of their greatest competitive advantages is found in their people's authentic voices, that tell the world what it's really like to work there.

To leaders: if you've held onto traditional views about brand-building being risky or self-serving, you have a real opportunity here. Consider asking better questions: How can we help our people show up more fully and authentically? How might their professional growth actually enhance our reputation, culture, and reach? What would it look like if our employees became our biggest advocates?

Support your team in building their brands, and you'll see returns in engagement, retention, visibility, and trust. These are the exact qualities that separate thriving organizations from struggling ones.

YOUR BRAND, YOUR CAREER, YOUR FUTURE

Throughout this book, we've tried to let you in on the truth that you already have a brand. The only question is whether you'll own it intentionally or let others define it for you.

We've seen what happens when talented professionals take control of their narrative. They stop waiting for permission to share their expertise. They build genuine relationships instead of transactional networks. They align their work with their values and see both their impact and income grow. And they build a stronger brand and attract better talent to the organization they work for.

The future belongs to people and organizations who understand that personal brands and organizational success are not in competition with each other, but are complementary. When employees feel empowered to share their authentic professional selves, everyone wins. Companies get genuine advocates; leaders attract top talent; individuals build careers aligned with who they really are.

So the choice is yours. You can keep your head down and hope someone notices your good work, or you can step into your full professional potential and show the world what you're capable of. Your brand is waiting: your career is calling. Your future, as yet, is unwritten.

What story will you tell?

PS: If you are a leader who wants to teach and inspire your employees to build their personal brands and share more content on LinkedIn, reach out to us and let's talk about working together to make that happen. You can find us on LinkedIn or our website, ownyourbrandbook.com

At the end of each chapter, we've provided reflection questions to help you apply these ideas to your specific situation. As usual, you can find these exercises and more in our free workbook at ownyourbrandbook.com.

Leaders: We talked about how organizations evolve from restricting employee visibility to partnering with them. Think about your current company or team:

- What stage are we in—restriction, permission, or partnership?

- How does our culture respond when someone builds a voice or presence outside the company?

- What's one small, specific action I could take that creates value both for me and my organization?

For Current and Aspiring Leaders: We also discussed how leaders can attract talent by showing up publicly and consistently. Think about the leaders you've followed or admired online:

- What made their presence stand out to you?

- What's one idea or philosophy I could highlight in my own LinkedIn profile or posts?

- How often do I engage publicly in ways that reflect the kind of leader I want to be?

WHY YOUR BRAND IS NEVER "FINISHED"

There are three types of people who finish reading a book like this.

The first type finishes the book and quickly moves onto the next without taking a single action to improve their personal brand. Not even a single post. You could make the argument that this group has wasted their time.

The second type might take a few actions like updating their LinkedIn profile, posting a few times, and maybe even landing a better job, but then they stop. They treat personal branding like a project with a clear beginning, middle, and end.

The third type understands that what they've just learned is the foundation for a practice that will evolve throughout their entire career. They understand this is a journey of continuous iteration and not just a destination. They understand the world of work will keep changing, that they must adapt and change along with it, and that building a personal brand is a never-ending pursuit.

The second group might see short-term gains, but the third group builds something that compounds over decades. They're the ones whose names come up in conversations they're not even part of; they're the ones who get opportunities they didn't apply for; and they're the ones whose brands become genuine assets that open doors automatically.

We hope you'll opt for the third option and continue building your brand for the rest of your career.

Like any journey, there are bound to be changes, challenges—and perhaps even pivots along the way. Your brand is supposed to change, because you're going to grow as a person. You'll develop new skills, and gain fresh insights. Your career goals will evolve, and your life circumstances will change. The industry you work in will transform in ways you can't predict today. What works for you at your current level may not serve you at the next level.

A word of encouragement: change is part of the system. Mike's brand today looks nothing like it did when he started building his first business. Back then, he was figuring out basic marketing principles and building confidence in his ability to help small businesses. Today, he's a recognized expert helping established professionals build sustainable personal brands. His core message about authenticity has remained consistent, but everything else, including his positioning, content, and target audience, has matured along with his expertise.

The same is true for Andy. When he started in corporate consulting and training, his brand was built around being a reliable, curious learner who could execute well. As he moved into independent consulting and speaking, it evolved to focus on helping professionals take ownership of their careers. After his cancer diagnosis and his family's move to Spain, it expanded to include themes of resilience and living intentionally. Each evolution built on what came before, but none of them were predetermined.

This is the reality of owning your brand in a sustainable, authentic way. The goal isn't to pinpoint the perfect positioning and stick with it forever.

So how do you build a brand that grows with you instead of constraining you? Simple: treat your personal brand as an iterative process rather than a fixed outcome. Here's how the process works:

1. **Try things.** Take what you've learned from this book and put it into practice. Update your LinkedIn profile, start sharing content, start those networking conversations, and apply for that stretch role. Don't wait until you have it all figured out—start with what you know right now.

2. **Reflect.** After you've been putting yourself out there for a few months, step back and assess: What's working? What isn't? How do you feel about the way you're showing up? Are you getting the kinds of opportunities you want? Do people understand what you're

about? Is there alignment between who you are and how you're being perceived?

3. **Adjust.** Based on your reflection, what needs to change? Maybe your content isn't resonating because it's too broad. Maybe you're attracting opportunities in the wrong direction. Maybe you're playing it too safe, or maybe you're being inauthentic to get attention. Make specific adjustments to your approach.

4. **Try again.** Implement your adjustments and see what happens. Make small, thoughtful changes based on real feedback and results.

5. **Repeat.** This cycle never ends! Even when you've built a strong, recognizable brand, you'll continue to iterate as you grow, as your industry changes, and as new opportunities emerge.

The good things happen in the repetition. Each cycle makes you more self-aware, more strategic, and more confident. You'll develop an intuition for what works and what doesn't; you'll build a track record of authentic content and meaningful relationships. Most importantly, you'll create a brand that feels genuinely *like you* because it's been shaped by your real experiences and reflections.

STRATEGIC THINKING: VERTICAL VS. HORIZONTAL GROWTH

As your career evolves, you'll face a recurring strategic question that directly impacts your personal brand: should you go deeper in your current area or broader across multiple areas? Understanding this choice—what we call vertical vs. horizontal focus—will help you position your brand more effectively during transitions.

Vertical focus means deepening your expertise within a specific industry or domain. If you're in healthcare marketing, vertical growth might look like this: healthcare marketing coordinator → healthcare marketing manager → healthcare brand strategist → VP of marketing for a healthcare company. You're staying within your vertical but advancing upward.

The advantage of vertical focus is credibility. When you speak about healthcare marketing challenges, people know you understand the regulatory constraints, buying cycles, and stakeholder dynamics. You become the go-to person for that specific intersection of skill and industry.

Horizontal focus means applying your core skills across different industries or contexts. If you're a project manager, horizontal growth might look like: project management in healthcare → project management in tech → project management in finance → consulting on project management best practices across industries.

The brand advantage of horizontal focus is versatility. You become known for your ability to take proven methodologies and adapt them to new environments. You bring fresh perspectives because you've seen how other industries solve similar problems.

Both approaches can build powerful personal brands, but they require different positioning strategies. If you're going vertical, emphasize your industry knowledge, relationships, and understanding of sector-specific challenges. If you're going horizontal, emphasize your methodology, adaptability, and cross-pollination insights.

Many successful professionals combine both approaches over time. Early in your career, you might focus vertically to build credibility. Later, you might leverage that credibility to expand horizontally. Or you might start horizontally to discover what you're passionate about, then focus vertically once you find your niche.

The important thing is being intentional about your choice and aligning your brand positioning accordingly. Don't try to be both the deepest expert in your field and the most versatile generalist at the same time: at least not without a clear strategy for how those pieces fit together.

THE ACTION CURE FOR OVERTHINKING

There's something we need to address about confidence, because it's one of the biggest things that stops people from their goals and dreams: you don't *think* your way into confidence. You *act* your way into it.

We learned this lesson from a keynote speaker named

Eric Thomas, known as the "Hip Hop Preacher." He said something that changed how we think about putting yourself out there: "It's not who you are that holds you back, it's who you think you're not."

Most people get stuck because they don't feel qualified enough, experienced enough, or confident enough. They think they need more credentials, success stories, or expertise before they can begin sharing their insights or applying for bigger roles.

But what actually happens when you start putting yourself out there is that you quickly realize that most of what you feared wouldn't happen. That LinkedIn post doesn't get torn apart in the comments; that networking conversation doesn't expose you as a fraud; that presentation doesn't end your career. In fact, you usually get positive responses that surprise you.

Use this evidence to build a little more confidence, which enables you to take slightly bigger actions, which generates more evidence, which builds more confidence. It's a progressive, self-reinforcing cycle. Start with what you know right now. You don't need to feel ready: you just need to start.

Action leads to experience, and experience leads to confidence. And so you have to start with action before building the confidence to show up regularly. And if you're scared to start, you're not alone. Just remember that courage is not the lack of fear, but recognizing fear and taking action anyway.

As you iterate and evolve over time, it's helpful to understand what should change and what should stay consistent.

What should evolve:

- Your expertise areas as you develop new skills and knowledge
- Your content topics as you learn new things and face new challenges
- Your positioning as you advance in your career or change directions
- Your goals as your life circumstances and priorities shift

What should stay consistent:

- Your core values and what you stand for
- Your authentic voice and communication style
- Your fundamental approach to building relationships
- Your integrity and character

The most powerful personal brands have this quality: they feel both familiar and fresh. You recognize the person but you can see how they've grown. They usually haven't become someone different; they've just become more fully themselves.

Remember: you can't "complete" your personal brand. It's a practice you have to maintain. Every interaction, every piece of content, and every career move adds a new chapter. You have everything you need to start. You don't have everything you need to finish, though, because there is no finish line. That's exactly what makes this exciting.

Your next iteration starts now. What will you try first?

At ownyourbrandbook.com, you'll find the complete workbook with every exercise from this book, plus bonus templates and reflection prompts you won't find anywhere else.

Your future self will thank you for taking action today instead of waiting until "someday." The career you want isn't going to build itself, but with the right tools and mindset, it's absolutely within reach.

Start your next iteration now.

ACKNOWLEDGEMENTS

ANDY WOULD LIKE TO THANK:

I want to start by thanking Mike for asking me to write this book with him and for being a great mentor and friend before this project. I've learned so much from you about building a personal brand and was so excited to do this with you and learn more along the way.

To the many mentors and friends who have taught me and supported me, and especially those I interviewed for this book: Lea Turner, Liam Darmody, Mita Mallick, Kait LeDonne, Travis Dommert, Darren McKee, Jessica Lorimer, Dr. Sergey Gorbatov, Gemma Stow, Lauren V. Davis, Massimo Backus, as well as others I've spoken with and mentioned: Larry McAllister, Brittany Honor, Jess Almlie, Rashi Kakkar, Kay Fabella, Keith Ferrazzi, Dr. Keith Keating, Amit Parmer, and others.

My great friend, Bennett Phillips, for always believing in me, supporting me, and encouraging me as well as giving me my first break into entrepreneurship and co-hosting a conference with me! I wouldn't be here without you.

Jon Hodge, for supporting and even funding my crazy ideas to build a brand, including starting the Talent Development Hot Seat and the first ever Talent Development Think Tank conference.

My International Mastermind crew whom I learn from on a regular basis: Bob Gentle, Lauren V. Davis, Joseph Bojang, Valerie Morris, Pete Everitt, Alex Curtis, Philip VanDusen, and Lee Matthew Jackson.

My wife, Cortney, and my amazing children, Lucy and Teddy, for supporting me, loving me, teasing me, and just being there with me every step of the way.

MIKE WOULD LIKE TO THANK:

Andy: I'm grateful we did this together. I deeply respect and admire how you've built your life, career, and family, and you were genuinely fun to collaborate with throughout this entire journey. Here's to many more.

Ann Ahn: You gave me my first real shot in my career, especially during a time of major transitions in my life. So much of what I learned about work, family, and life came from you, and I still carry those lessons with me today. Thank you for seeing something in me before I could see it myself.

Henry Jeong: A brother in every sense of the word. Your insights, reviews, and constant help made this book immeasurably better. Thank you for your friendship.

Mom: Your belief in my unconventional path gave me permission to explore until I found work that truly fits. This book exists because you let me be exactly who I needed to be.

My nephews, Haru and Taeho: One memory that always finds its way back to me is taking pictures of you when you were really little with my first book. Here we are now on my third. I hope a fulfilling livelihood will reveal itself to you as it did to Uncle Mike. For now, keep playing fútbol. Or better yet, play for a living, that would be fun.

My sister Esther: Life post-40 has been wild and yet so fun and fulfilling, thanks in large part to you always cheering me on. Your support means everything.

Dad: You read my other books, and I'm sad you won't read this one. I told you this right before you passed, but I'll say it again here: I remember you making me read newspapers as a kid and listening to vocabulary tapes in your car. Because of those foundations, I've been able to do what I do. Rest in peace.

To God: Thank you for this amazing life.

ABOUT THE AUTHORS

Andy Storch is a keynote speaker and author of two books, including *Own Your Brand, Own Your Career* and *Own Your Career, Own Your Life*, who is on a mission to teach and inspire more people to build their brands, own their careers, and prepare for the future.

Andy is the host of two podcasts, including the Talent Development Hot Seat and the Own Your Career Show, as well as the founder and host of the Talent Development Think Tank conference and community.

He has spoken on stages and facilitated workshops on

five continents for professionals across multiple industries, on topics including owning your career, achieving goals, building your brand, improving performance, and modern leadership.

Most importantly, Andy is a husband and father on a mission to get the most out of life and inspire others to do the same.

Mike Kim is a personal brand strategist who helps executives, experts, and entrepreneurs build authentic personal brands that create opportunities and accelerate careers. He understands how to help talented people get noticed, get heard, and get ahead by learning to communicate their value clearly and consistently.

Mike came out of a career in marketing and has spent over a decade helping professionals transition from "talented underdogs" to recognized authorities in their fields. His refreshing, authentic approach has made him a sought-after speaker, online educator, and consultant. Mike's clients include industry leaders who've been featured on major platforms including PBS, TED, CNN, and Fox.

Mike has been featured in and written for *Inc.*, *Entrepreneur*, and *The Huffington Post*. He is the author of the *Wall Street Journal* and *USA Today* bestselling book *You Are the Brand: The 8-Step Blueprint to Showcase Your Unique Expertise and Build a Highly Profitable, Personally Fulfilling Business.*

He has spoken at industry-leading events including Social Media Marketing World, Tribe Conference, and Podcast Movement, and has been a guest on leading podcasts like *Smart Passive Income*, *Entrepreneurs on Fire*, and *Read to Lead*. For more, visit mikekim.com.

www.ingramcontent.com/pod-product-compliance
Lightning Source LLC
LaVergne TN
LVHW051047080426
835508LV00019B/1754